Succulents
and Cactus

By the Sunset Editorial Staff with Jack Kramer

Lane Books · Menlo Park, California

FOREWORD

Your first visit to a succulent and cactus nursery may amaze you with the extreme variety of plant types available. The cactus family, alone, has over 1,300 species; succulents can be found in many plant families, so that the number of species is well more than double the number for cactus. To be sure, many of these plants are botanical curiosities, representing nature's ingenuity in adapting plants to environmental extremes; yet these same oddities, when used properly, can become the exclamation points in more conventional gardens.

The objective of this book is to give you down-to-earth advice on the care of succulents and cactus—both indoors and out—and to suggest a variety of possibilities for their use. The miniaturist can find limitless ways to derive pleasure growing the smaller kinds indoors, while the outdoor gardener can fit both large and small ones into almost any garden scheme. The fancier of colorful exotic flowers can find an abundance of different plants which will produce blooms to surprise and delight the eye. We hope this book will be your inspiration to look into the vast and varied world of succulents and cactus.

Edited by Philip Edinger

PHOTOGRAPHERS

Molly Adams: 77 (top). **William Aplin:** 4 (bottom), 11 (bottom), 17 (top right), 35 (right), 40, 44 (left), 46, 48, 49 (top), 50 (bottom), 52 (bottom), 53 (bottom right), 54 (bottom), 55 (top), 61 (top) 71 (bottom), 74, 76 (bottom), 77 (bottom). **Aplin-Dudley Studios:** 17 (bottom), 53 (bottom left). **Ernest Braun:** 25, 39 (top), 55 (bottom). **William D. Carter:** Cover. **Clyde Childress:** 21 (bottom), 29 (right), 45. **Glenn M. Christiansen:** 7, 38 (bottom), 43 (bottom left), 51 (bottom right), 71 (top), 79 (bottom). **Nancy Davidson:** 50 (top). **Richard Dawson:** 8 (bottom left), 15 (bottom), 27 (bottom), 29 (left), 52 (top), 53 (top). **Don Erskine:** 15 (top). **Richard Fish:** 5, 8 (bottom right), 10 (top), 11 (top), 13 (bottom), 51 (bottom left). **Frank L. Gaynor:** 42. **Jeannette Grossman:** 43 (top). **Hort-Pix:** 73 (bottom left). **Art Hupy:** 43 (bottom right). **Eric Johnson:** 44 (right). **Eeda Johnstone:** 79 (top). **Elsa Knoll:** 37 (bottom), 41 (bottom). **Roy Krell:** 27 (top). **Ells Marugg:** 69 (top). **Jack McDowell:** 64, 65, 66, 67. **Don Normark:** 10 (bottom), 21 (top), 28 (right), 31 (bottom), 35 (left), 47 (top). **Ken & Gerrie Reichard:** 33 (top), 69 (bottom), 73. **John Robinson:** 39 (bottom), 49 (bottom left), 54 (top). **Martha Rosman:** 33 (bottom), 76 (top). **Blair Stapp:** 38 (top). **USDA Photo:** 6, 34. **Darrow Watt:** 4 (top), 12, 13 (top), 16, 17 (top left), 24, 26, 30 (top), 31 (top), 36, 37 (top), 41 (top), 47 (bottom), 49 (bottom right), 56, 57, 58, 59, 60, 61 (bottom), 63, 70. **R. Wenkam:** 30 (bottom), 68. **Williams Photography:** 78. **Joyce R. Wilson:** 20. **Steven C. Wilson:** 28 (left).

FRONT COVER: Luminous color and sculptural form are displayed by this 16-inch rosette of *Dudleya brittonii*. Foliage in the background belongs to another succulent, *Crassula argentea*—the familiar jade plant. Photograph by William D. Carter. Illustrations by Adrian Martinez.

Executive Editor, Sunset Books: David E. Clark

Ninth Printing November 1974

CONTENTS

SPECIAL FEATURES

GLISTENING WHITE, 10-inch flowers on terminal growth characterize Trichocereus spachianus; sharp spines are yellow, plant is shiny green, ribbed.

DISTINCTIVE LANDSCAPE PICTURE is created with barrel cactus (Echinocactus grusonii) and old man cactus (Cephalocereus senilis). Barrels may reach 4 feet high, 2½ feet across.

An Introduction to Succulents and Cactus

Amazing variety of colors and shapes in the foliage and flowers

There is a hidden treasure of plants waiting for you when you look into the world of succulents and cactus. Here is a wealth of plant material to turn a barren landscape into an unusual garden or a bright window into a showcase of colorful foliage and flowers. If you are an apartment dweller and space is limited,

PORCELAIN-LIKE aeonium spills into planting of Korean grass, the texture contrast enhancing both plants. Over 50 rosettes grow in this area not more than 3 feet square.

decorative dish gardens can give you miniature desert scenes indoors. In all-year temperate climates, big plants like the organpipe cactus (*Lemaireocereus thurberi*) or some of the aloes and agaves can be put in the ground for permanent landscape features. Where summers are short, these same plants are suitable container subjects.

The variety of plant forms is infinite. You can grow different kinds for striking foliage, for individualistic plant shapes, or for colorful flowers; often these different features may be found combined in a single plant. Echeverias have foliage in shades of blue-green or pale green, often lined with red or pink; some plants (like *Euphorbia grandicornis*) have bizarre shapes; other types are desirable because of the interesting patterns of the spines. If you are fond of flowers, the beautiful orchid and Christmas cacti are perennial favorites, while night-blooming types with breathtaking 12-inch flowers offer dramatic beauty.

A cactus is simply a succulent plant that can store moisture, but not all succulents are cactus. Succulents do not belong to any one plant family but are represented in nearly thirty different ones. You find them in the lily, amaryllis, crassula, daisy, and milkweed families, and even among the geraniums.

You can easily identify cactus. With rare exceptions (the lemon vine, *Pereskia aculeata*, and its close relatives) they do not have leaves or, when any are present they soon fall. Although most of them have spines and bristles, there are even some cactus without spines; several have long hair or a wooly covering instead.

Among the succulents, the often-seen jade plant (*Crassula argentea*) and the donkey tail (*Sedum morganianum*) have been popular house plants for years because they grow almost untended. The crown-of-thorns (*Euphorbia milii*) and the poinsettia (*Euphorbia pulcherrima*) have withstood the test of time as beautiful gift plants. The familiar wax plant (*Hoya carnosa*) is a succulent and so is the rosary vine (*Ceropegia woodii*). Tiny crassulas and sedums that you have seen for years in florist shop windows are also part of this large group.

PROMINENT FEATURE of southwest deserts is the saguaro (Carnegiea gigantea); slow growing, garden and container specimens will remain unbranched like the saguaro at the far right.

From Many Lands and Climates

Although the deserts of the world have many succulents, not all succulents are desert plants. They exist in jungles, on mountains, and near lakes and seas. The semi-arid regions of North and South America, Asia, and Africa all have succulents, but many also dwell in the rain forests. In mountains there are succulents that thrive despite bitter cold, strong winds, and poor soil.

The cactus family ranges from Canada in the north through Central America and the West Indies and south to the cold areas of Chile and Patagonia. Perhaps Mexico has the richest collection of cactus, but many are also found in the western deserts of the United States and high in the Cordilleras of Peru, Bolivia, and Argentina.

Distinctive Foliage, Plant Forms

The diversified forms and colorings of succulents are beautiful, sometimes bizarre, but always interesting. *Cotyledon undulata* looks like pale green, delicately-carved porcelain. Some of the euphorbias appear to have exploded to produce their contorted shapes. Many kalanchoes and gasterias derive their popularity from handsome mottled foliage, while the sculptural quality of sword-shaped aloes and agaves provide material of striking interest indoors or out.

The echeveria species deserve special mention for their wide variety of sizes and shapes—from miniatures to low-branched shrubs to plants with a single rosette of leaves atop a stem. The colors and textures of the leaves—every shade of green dusted with red or purple, or frosty white with tinges of pink or blue—make them highly desirable as indoor decoration or as a focal point in an otherwise green planting in the garden.

The bright green, rubbery leaves of *Crassula argentea* have given it the name jade plant, while *C. arborescens* has silvery foliage dotted and margined red. St. Andrew's Cross *(C. treibneri)* is well-known for its pale yellow-green leaves that arrange themselves in a perfect cross; the rattle-

POLKA-DOT APPEARANCE of Opuntia microdasys albispina *is produced by tufts of white spines on oval, flattened pads to 6 inches across.*

WEATHERED ROCK provides good texture contrast to the delicately scalloped leaves of Cotyledon undulata (left) and rosettes of Grapto-petalum paraguayense.

PRICKLY PEAR FLOWERS are 6-8 inches across, fragile-looking in contrast to the spiny plants.

CONTRAST IN TEXTURE, form between soft leaves of Kalanchoe beharensis (top) and spiny aloe (front).

snake crassula *(C. teres)* carries its leaves in a tightly packed column.

If it is white leaves you want, look at the amazing chalk lettuce *(Dudleya pulverulenta)* or some of the smaller types like *D. candida* and *D. farinosa.* Surely, you would think someone had doused them with white paint.

Kalanchoes are frequent household favorites. Included in this group are the panda plant *(K. tomentosa)* with silvery plush leaves stained red at the margins and the pen wiper plant *(K. marmorata)* with its heavily spotted gray-green leaves.

Sedums offer a bewildering variety in form and color. The cockscomb sedum, dragon blood sedum, the donkey tail are a few examples of their descriptive names. The sempervivums are brilliantly colored with leaves tinted crimson or purple or edged in red. Some aeoniums have nearly black foliage tinted coppery or bronze-red.

Succulents, with the exception of some euphorbias and a few aloes and agaves, do not have harmful spines and can be handled easily without personal risk. The velvet-leafed kinds like echeverias do require some care when you touch them because the powdery coating on the leaves is easily bruised.

Cactus, in their struggle to survive, have become —with few exceptions—leafless plants with ribbed or flattened bodies, the stems taking over from the leaves the process of manufacturing food. Their distinctive shapes—balls, melons, globes, barrels —are well known. Their spines are well known, too, (some plants must be handled with gloves), but within the patterns created by the spines is often much of their beauty.

While it is true that almost any cactus has spines, not all spines are so hard and needle-like that they will cut you when you touch them. Many species bear soft furry spines that feel like velvet, and there are others with long spines that are soft and pliable and cannot break the skin. Generally, the species that are treacherous are grown for their unique forms and are more for collectors than for the average hobbyist. Most often, these are large plants, not suitable for indoor culture. The majority of cactus for indoor gardens—rebutia, notocactus, chamaecereus, lobivia, parodia, epiphyllum and rhipsalis—do not have formidable spines and can be handled safely. Plants from the strombocactus, stenocactus, and coryphantha groups, however, generally do have sharp spines.

Outdoors, large cactus like the organ pipe and torch types provide attractive backgrounds for smaller varieties; even a window sill of barrel cactus can be effective. Striking landscape accents can be provided by those species that have colorful spines. The golden barrel cactus *(Echinocactus grusonii)* has yellow spines decorating a bright green globe; *E. horizonthalonius* features pink or red spines on a silver-gray body. For close-up appreciation there are a number of cactus with novel forms: *Opuntia microdasys* carries its flattened pads in an arrangement that imitates a rabbit's profile, mammillarias resemble pincushions, while the old man cactus *(Cephalocereus senilis)* is covered with white wooly hair.

Flowers: From Subtle to Startling

If you have ever seen the desert in bloom you will remember the spectacle for a long time. This array of color—delicate yellow, vibrant red, explosive purple, and pure white—is all part of nature's palette in the cactus family. While blooms may not be as prevalent on indoor plants as they are in the landscape, with good selection and care many cactus species will reward you with flowers. The colors are often bright and gaudy, perhaps a consolation for the flowers' short lives: Generally they last only a few days.

For their plant sizes, many cactus have mammoth flowers. Rebutia, notocactus, and opuntia often bear 3 to 4-inch flowers on 6 to 8-inch plants. Most cactus blooms are open-faced with delicate petals; some are frilly and daisy-like, or silken-textured with numerous petals and sepals grading into one another. Even the ways in which flowers are displayed vary from one kind to another. Mammilarias, for example, have a crown of color—a perfect circle around the top—while some rebutias have flowers at the base. Although some cactus flower only at night, most species open their flowers during the daytime.

Several cactus (like opuntia) will not bloom until they reach a certain age, but most kinds will bloom indoors without your waiting many years to see their flowers. It is true that a great deal of sun and heat are required by some species, but many others bloom with ordinary container care. Rebutias, for example, provide abundant color at an early age.

Most of the smaller cactus plants produce flowers more readily than the larger types. Rebutias, again, are a prime example. Often, a 1-inch plant will bear several 2 to 3-inch brilliant blooms, completely covering the top of the plant in a cloud of color. Most succulents and cactus are spring and

SEEMINGLY FASHIONED FROM STONE, this blue-white, spiny agave nestles in a bed of Sedum rubrotinctum.

LIVING TAPESTRY is created by sempervivum species growing from soil pocket in crevice of this rock.

summer blooming, but by selecting the right varieties you can also have color in fall and winter.

In succulents, fig-marigolds or ice plants are stunning in their flowering season and make sheets of color. The bright flowers of agaves and aloes on tall spikes are impressive, while the wax-plant (Hoya carnosa) gracefully displays exotic waxy-white blooms in clusters on a vine-like plant. Euphorbia flowers are usually inconspicuous, becoming showy only when surrounded by colorful bracts as in the poinsettia, E. pulcherrima.

Choice Governs Success

Succulents and cactus have been popular through the years because — if necessary — they will adapt to low indoor humidity; most need little water to survive. However, even though most of these plants can endure drought, remember that not all of them prefer it. If you know what part of the world a plant comes from and something about the climate of that area, you can select the right plants for the conditions you can offer them. A tree-growing epiphyte that is accustomed to high humidity and ample moisture will not respond to desert conditions. Conversely, a desert dweller will have a tough time adjusting to shady, moist areas. Before you select plants, determine what kind of growing conditions you have. Put your succulents and cactus where they will have a fighting chance and they will be with you for years.

GRACEFUL CANDELABRAS of bright red flowers arise from a stiff, toothed rosette in Aloe ferox.

TRANSLUCENT GREEN LEAVES of Agave attenuata look more dangerous than they really are: Spines are soft, bend to the touch. Foreground planting is yellow-flowered sedum with bronzy foliage.

Starting a Collection

Selection and placement of plants are of prime importance

VARIOUS SHAPES AND COLORS of foliage abound in this greenhouse collection of succulents.

Because there are so many succulents and cactus, you should know something about them before you shop for plants. Study the photographs and lists in this book, suppliers' catalogues, then try to decide which plants you want. Some plants are truly outstanding, many of them are more bizarre than beautiful, and a few are simply oddities.

If you have a chance to visit a succulents and cactus nursery, you can be sure of your selections. Look for specimens that have good color and form, abundant bloom, and vigor. Start your collection with whatever plants appeal to you; sooner or later, you may find a particular group that will interest you more than others.

Flower shows often contain displays of succulents and cactus which will also help acquaint you with the variety of flowers and plants available to the collector.

When You Shop for Plants . . .

Succulents and cactus are available from mail order suppliers, at local nurseries, or from friends. If you order by mail, start with a few plants; when these plants prove themselves to be satisfactory, then you can order more with confidence. Usually you will find that mail order suppliers are reputable. In comparison, bargain counters at dime stores and supermarkets are a gamble: Often plants sold there are newly-collected or recently-replanted and are going through a critical re-adjustment period under unfavorable conditions. Such plants may be difficult for you to establish. Stock

LETTUCE-LIKE ROSETTES of wavy leaves shaded with red, bronze, or purple are characteristic of many echeveria hybrids, well-displayed in shallow dishes.

GIANT TOOTHED SWORDS of this century plant (Agave americana marginata) give emphasis to a bed of aeonium (foreground) and sedum.

from mail order suppliers will usually come in pots in which the plants have already been established before shipment.

Today, local nurseries often have many succulents and cactus. These plants generally will be small but excellent for beginners. If you do some hunting in your community and have a sharp eye, you may be amazed at what you can find in local greenhouses.

You may want large plants if you plan to landscape with succulents and cactus. To receive these plants in good condition (if you order them by mail) there are a few rules you should observe. First, order them in pots rather than bare root. Upon arrival they will have to adjust to new conditions and that is enough of a problem at the start. Later, they can be transplanted. If you are fortunate the plants will be in plastic pots which will reduce shipping costs. Many times, however, they will have been grown in oil cans; even so, it is better to leave them in their containers and repot later, after plants have become accustomed to their new environment. Too often, bare root succulents or cactus fail to re-establish after shipment.

For long distances have plants sent Air Parcel Post; for short trips, shipment by bus is satisfactory. In most cases you will have to pick up the plants, but it is better for the plants if you get them immediately rather than waiting a few days for delivery.

Spring and fall are the best times to buy succulents and cactus from mail order suppliers. In the winter, weather is too uncertain, and in summer even more new plants will succumb to heat than might perish in low winter temperatures.

How to Handle New Plants

Your plants—whether they come from a mail order house or a local nursery—need more care in the first few weeks with you than at any other time: It takes them a few weeks to adjust to new conditions. Do not put plants in direct sun after they have traveled in closed boxes. Put them in an indirectly lighted place for a few days; then move them into more light. Moderate watering is all they need during this period.

When you receive new arrivals be sure they are free from insects. Immerse the pot halfway in a tub of water for a few hours; you may be surprised at how many uninvited guests appear on the soil surface. Even the best regulated nurseries occasionally have their share of pests.

Proper Location is Vital

Succulents and cactus are tantalizing; the collector always wants more plants, until suddenly he finds himself without adequate space for them. At that moment it is easy to let enthusiasm tempt you into placing plants in less-favorable environments. Inevitably, this will lead to disappointment: These plants languish and die in dark or shaded areas.

Generally, most indoor succulents and cactus need a window with sun or bright light. Rather than placing a few plants at several windows, try to put them all in one area; then it is easier to water them and keep them groomed. If you need large plants to accent a shaded corner, make provisions for artificial light in that area (see page 35).

If plants are to be grown outdoors, be especially careful when you select them. If you are not sure they will be hardy in your climate, don't put them in the ground; grow them in containers so they can be moved inside when frost threatens. Of course, you can experiment: A great many succulents and cactus will tolerate cool nights and temperatures slightly above freezing.

Decorative Accents—Inside or Out

Small plants are the best choices for windows where space is limited. A conglomeration of large plants in a small area creates an untidy picture. Haworthias, rebutias, and the smaller agaves and aloes are good window subjects.

Use potted plants on garden walls or ledges—or any place where decoration is needed. Large tubs brimming with echeverias or a specimen agave in a distinctive container make handsome wall plants. Choose hanging species, too, like *Sedum morganianum,* to drape a wall with color and distinctive patterns.

For spectacular ground covers, don't overlook the numerous ice plant species formerly classified as mesembryanthemums (see p. 74). These are inexpensive, rewarding plants which cover an area quickly. When they bloom—and many do abundantly—it can be a blanket of bright color. Some of the hardy sedums are equally fine choices for ground covers, requiring little care.

A garden of succulents and cactus in containers grouped together can be attractive and colorful with foliage and flowers. Use large aeoniums for round tubs, echerevias for shallow dishes, or perhaps a specimen agave in a pedestal urn. This is a portable garden that can be rearranged at will and taken inside in cold weather.

*SOFT YELLOW FLOWERS rise above
shiny green rosettes of Aeonium
holochrysum. Mature rosettes may
measure 15-18 inches across.*

*GOOD DISPLAY AREA for collection of succulents and cactus is low wall or shelf against sunny fence.
Plants are not only easy to see but are also easy to care for, may be rearranged at any time.*

BRILLIANT CLUSTERS of red, orange, yellow, or salmon flowers decorate Kalanchoe blossfeldiana *hybrids.*

An outdoor planter can be yet another show-place for low-maintenance succulents and cactus. Tall opuntias and rosette agaves, shrubby crassulas and compact haworthias are all reliable outdoor display plants.

On a wall, in a planter, on the terrace or patio—in containers or in the ground there are all kinds of succulents and cactus to beautify your home and landscape.

Colorful Flowers are provided by these species and hybrids. With some, the color impact comes from masses of flowers in bloom at one time; others have individual flowers that are large and captivating.

Echeveria derenbergii
Echinocactus horizonthalonius
Echinopsis (many hybrids)
Epiphyllum (many hybrids)
Huernia keniensis
Kalanchoe blossfeldiana
Lobivia aurea
Lobivia haageana
Mammillaria baumii
Mammillaria hahniana
Notocactus mammulosus
Notocactus ottonis
Opuntia microdasys
Parodia aureispina
Rebutia miniscula
Schlumbergera (many hybrids)
Stapelia variegata
Zygocactus (many hybrids)

Striking Foliage in many different shapes and color arrangements are represented in this list of popular succulents.

Aeonium canariense
Agave stricta
Agave victoriae-reginae
Aloe aristata
Aloe striata
Cotyledon orbiculata
Crassula argentea
Echeveria pulvinata
Haworthia margaritifera
Kalanchoe beharensis
Kleinia articulata
Rebutia kupperiana
Sansevieria 'Hahnii'
Sedum morganianum
Senecio crassissimus

BUFF-YELLOW STARFISH is a 10-inch flower of Stapelia nobilis; *plant is like spineless, columnar cactus.*

CHALK LETTUCE (Dudleya pulverulenta) *is good fore-ground plant, nearly glows against dark background*

MISTY GRAY-GREEN overlaid with a silvery-white powder: this is Dudleya brittonii. Leaves are brittle, so place it away from traffic.

DESCRIPTIVE GUIDE TO FAVORITE GENERA

On these two pages are listed the most widely-grown genera of succulents and cactus. Each genus will usually contain a number of species (and perhaps some named hybrids), differing from one another in certain details but resembling one another more than they would resemble species in any other genus. From this list you can determine *general* characteristics which will help you estimate which groups of plants may be best suited to the space and conditions you have.

Succulents

Aeonium. This is a group of shrubby plants having woody stems crowned with rosettes of succulent leaves. Plants die after flowering but usually produce offshoots to form new plants. Native to Africa, the Canary and Madeira islands.

Agave. These are strongly-formed plants belonging to the amaryllis family. Large species are bold landscape subjects; smaller ones are attractive container plants indoors or out. Leaves are sword shaped, often toothed, and carried in rosettes. They bloom infrequently in cultivation and die thereafter. Native to the Americas.

Aloe. Many of the aloes with fleshy, pointed leaves arranged in rosettes resemble agaves. These plants, however, belong to the lily family and have showy flowers which are produced with great regularity. There are small or medium-sized species for indoor culture and giants for the permanent landscape. Although the biggest show of flowers is from February to September, some species will be in bloom every month of the year. Leaves are often banded or streaked with contrasting colors. Native to Africa, the Mediterranean, and Atlantic islands.

Cotyledon. Growth types include shrubby plants with thick rounded leaves covered with whitish powder and several low-growing sorts with fleshy, pointed leaves. Some cotyledons shed their foliage every year while others have persistent leaves. Native to semi-arid regions in Africa.

Crassula. This is a large genus of usually small-to-medium-sized plants. Their fleshy leaves are arranged in a number of patterns, depending upon the species; some have branching stems while others are low plants with dense foliage. These are generally not spectacular but are versatile and dependable. Mostly native to South Africa.

Dudleya. Best known species are rosette-shaped with beautiful chalky-white leaves; species with finger-like leaves are also found in the genus. Plants are short stemmed or flat on the ground. Native to coastal California and Mexico.

Echeveria. Rosette succulents with fleshy leaves of green or gray-green, often marked or overlaid with deeper colors. Flowers are bell-shaped and nodding, usually pink, red, or yellow, in clusters on long, slender stems. Growth habit ranges from spreading clumps to small shrubs with short stems. Many beautiful hybrids. Native to the Americas.

Euphorbia. See page 72.

Faucaria. Very fleshy triangular leaves are held in angular rosettes; plants are generally stemless. Leaves may be grayish or green, sometimes tinged with red and often spotted, while leaf margins are usually toothed. Daisy-like yellow or white flowers are large in proportion to the small plants. Native to South Africa.

Gasteria. These plants are related to aloes in the lily family, but the leaves are often blunt and held in a fan shape, although some species grow in rosettes, especially as they age. Characteristically, the leaves are dark green mottled with pale green or white; flowers are usually red and bell-shaped with green tips, borne along slender stems. Very durable plants, tolerant of shade and neglect. Native to South Africa.

Haworthia. Extremely variable in growth habit: Some of the best-known ones resemble the smaller aloes, but others make small towers of neatly stacked fleshy leaves or stemless rosettes. Leaf colors are also variable, from grayish through shades of green. Native to South Africa.

Kalanchoe. Native to tropical regions of America, Africa, and south-east Asia, this gives a clue to their general intolerance of frost and preference of moisture. Many species are known, usually with branching, shrubby plants. Leaves may be smooth or felted, flowers are often showy in shades of red through yellow.

Sansevieria. Thick, patterned leaves grow in clusters and radiate up and out from base; leaves range in shape from short, blunt triangles to long swords. These have been popular house plants for generations, able to survive with the most casual care: dry air, little light, uneven temperatures, and infrequent watering. Native to Africa and India.

Sedum. Some sedums are tiny and trailing, others are bushy and upright. All have fleshy leaves, but size, shape, and color are highly variable among the species, and some are even deciduous. Flowers are usually small and starlike, in moderately large clusters. The smaller sedums are useful in rock gardens, as ground or bank covers, or in small areas where unusual texture or color is needed. Larger kinds may be used as shrubs.

Sempervivum. Stemless plants have tightly-packed rosettes of leaves. Little offsets cluster around the parent rosette which dies after flowering, leaving the offsets to form new clumps. Flowers are not showy. All species and varieties need sun, good drainage, and generous summer watering. Native to the mountains of central and southern Europe, Asia Minor, and north Africa.

CACTUS

Astrophytum. Sea urchin cactus, bishop's cap, and goat-horn cactus are in this group. Usually globular shapes or with prominent ribs, some have a covering of wooly hair. These small plants are excellent indoors. Flowers are yellow to red.

Cephalocereus. The familiar old man cactus exemplifies this group: tall columnar or branching growth, usually covered by long, wooly hair. Most flower at night but only rarely indoors.

Cereus. Eventually these make tree-sized plants to 30 feet or more, but young ones are fine house plants. Large (to 8 inches) white flowers on old plants appear at night. Stems are blue-green.

Chamaecereus. Bright flowers in red shades will appear indoors on these small, clump-forming plants. Short shoots branch from the base to produce the clump effect.

Cleistocactus. In nature some species grow to 6 feet tall; all are recognizable by a definite narrowing of the stem near the growing point. Stems are usually no more than 1 inch thick, often leaning, and so thickly covered with spines that the stem surface is hardly visible. These are easy to grow, and the orange to red flowers are profuse.

Coryphantha. Globular or cylindrical plants (some as much as 12 inches high) with interesting spine patterns have large yellow, red, or purple flowers. Definite winter rest is required.

Echinocactus. Included here are the most familiar barrel sorts. These are heavily spined, produce flowers from near the crown of mature plants. Young plants are good container subjects; mature specimens may be several feet tall.

Echinocereus. Usually these are free-branching clusters or mounds of erect stems, sometimes prostrate, and usually less than a foot tall. All have highly ornamental spines which densely cover the plant surfaces. Showy flowers (to 4 inches across) are long-lasting.

Echinopsis. Small cylindrical or globular plants have definite vertical ribs. Flowers are long-tubed, many-petaled, in shades of white, yellow, pink, or red, and may reach 6-8 inches in length. These are among the least particular as to soil, amount of water, and light.

Epiphyllum. See pages 70-71.

Gymnocalycium. Plant bodies are usually globular with regularly arranged protrusions which give them the name "chin cactus". Flowers are red, pink, or white, on plants less than 10 inches high.

Lobivia. Small globular or cylindrical shapes with big, showy flowers in shades of red, yellow, pink, orange, purplish, lilac. Flowers are sometimes nearly as big as plants.

Mammillaria. Small, cylindrical or globe-shaped, these plants may be single-stemmed or clustered. Red, pink, yellow, or white flowers are usually small, arranged in a circle near the plant's top.

Notocactus. These are small ball cactus from South America, easily grown and free-flowering. Flowers are yellow or purplish-red.

Opuntia. This genus includes the prickly pears, beaver tail, and chollas. Generally it is divided into three groups based upon growth form: the prickly pears which have flat pads; the tall cylindrical chollas; and the short species with globe-shaped or cylindrical stems. Some make excellent landscape subjects, others are fine for window gardens. Most are free-flowering with white, yellow, orange, purple, or red blooms.

Parodia. These are small species similar to notocactus; they flower heavily, have decorative (usually curving) spines, and require little attention.

Rebutia. Small, globular species from high altitudes, these plants bear flowers from the sides or from around the base; flowers are large for size of plant.

Rhipsalis. These are epiphytic, trailing plants which require the same culture as epiphyllum (see page 70). Some species have flattened stems, but the majority have slender, cylindrical segments. Flowers are small and not showy.

Schlumbergera. See "Christmas Cactus", page 77.

Thelocactus. Small globular to cylindrical plants are notable for their especially decorative spines. Flowers are around 2 inches across, red, pink, yellow, or white, and appear at the plant's top.

Zygocactus. See "Christmas Cactus", page 77.

Caring for Succulents and Cactus

Requirements for healthy growth are easy to satisfy

GRAVEL MULCH on soil surface serves two purposes: plants' bases stay dry, soil can't splash on leaves.

After you have selected your plants and noted a few basic cultural steps, growing succulents and cactus is less work and more pleasure than is gardening with most other house plants. Their fleshy leaves are able to store great quantities of water if you forget to tend them. The leathery foliage is rarely attacked by insects—it is just too tough. Furthermore, if you do mistreat a plant, you will find it has tremendous recuperative powers.

LIGHT REQUIREMENTS

Good light is essential for the best growth of succulents and cactus; therefore it is wise to select plants according to your window space and available natural light. Choose only those kinds that can be expected to succeed in the environments you can provide.

Although optimum conditions are always desirable, some plants will—if they must—adjust to less-than-favorable environments. In such situations your plants will not grow as well or bloom as profusely as you might like, but they will survive. Light affects the color of foliage and the formation of flower buds. In sun, leaves have a strong color and there is abundant bloom; in dim light, plants are somewhat less colorful and flowering may be sparse, if at all.

Turn potted plants occasionally so that light reaches all parts of the foliage evenly. The exception to this is plants that are ready to bloom: Do not move them, as the change in light can cause buds to drop.

WHEN COLD WEATHER THREATENS, plastic panel sides of this greenhouse can be put on so that temperatures inside will not drop too low; sides are removed during warm weather for good air circulation.

POCKET-SIZED DESERT of succulents and cactus has gravel ground cover which provides mulch for plants in the ground, foil for those in containers.

SOIL PREFERENCES

Succulents and cactus do not grow in pure sand as is sometimes believed; they require a good nutritional soil. There are numerous possible soil mixtures, and what works well for one grower may not work well for another. Different climates play a part in the choice of soils. In weather that is consistently warm a loose, well-drained mixture is necessary for plants; in cooler weather where plants are not watered as much, a somewhat heavier soil gives better plant growth.

A mix composed of equal parts garden loam, leaf mold, and sand provides a satisfactory medium for most succulents. For cactus, add more sand and some gravel to the mix. Jungle species like epiphyllum and rhipsalis will thrive in a mixture of one part shredded fir bark or osmunda (available at nurseries) and one part garden loam. The ingredients must be thoroughly mixed and have a loose, friable texture so the medium will drain water easily yet offer moisture for plant roots.

Prepared soil bought from a local greenhouse will be thoroughly mixed and contain all necessary nutrients for plant growth. It also will have been sterilized so there is little chance for growth of weeds or bacteria. Packaged soil prepared especially for succulents and cactus is satisfactory, too; soil mixtures for African violets are generally too rich and heavy.

Soil mixes in large bags at nurseries may be suitable, but these usually will need more sand for desert plants. Soil-less or peatlike mixes—while lightweight and good for some plants—are not suitable for succulents and cactus. They contain no nutrients, so that a careful feeding program (which takes time) must be followed.

CONTAINER CULTURE

Succulents and cactus can be grown in many different containers: clay pots, wooden tubs or boxes, glazed pots, or even in pieces of rocks. Perhaps the most popular container is the standard terra cotta pot. It provides good drainage (promoting good soil aeration), is inexpensive, and comes in many sizes. However, plants in it will dry out faster than when grown in other types of pots, so more frequent watering is necessary.

Glazed pots (usually selected for their decorative appearance) can be used too, provided they have drainage holes. Plants in them must be watered with more care because moisture cannot escape from their sides. However, this can be an advantage whenever you are away from home for several days.

Plastic pots are often used because they are lightweight, neat, inexpensive, and come in a number of colors. They are easy to clean but have a tendency to tip over if they contain large plants.

Consider the size of the container in relation to the size of the plant being grown. Not only does a small plant look lost in a large pot, it rarely will thrive: Unused soil becomes waterlogged. Conversely, you cannot expect a large specimen to respond in a tiny pot. Generally, for round plants use a pot one or two inches wider than the diameter of the plant. For vertical specimens choose a pot half as wide as the plant is tall. Remember that small pots (under 4 inches in diameter) are difficult to care for—they dry out rapidly and the plants require frequent watering.

Potting and Repotting Hints

Scrub all pots—new or old—with hot water to be sure they are free of dirt and possible insect eggs. Soak clay pots overnight so they will not absorb the water that the plant needs. Remember always to use containers with drainage holes in the bottom. If you have a decorative container with no drainage hole you can plant your succulent or cactus in an ordinary clay pot which will fit *inside* the more attractive container. When you water this plant, however, you must be sure that the bottom of the clay pot won't be left standing in water. Either lift out the clay pot when you water, or empty extra water out of the decorative container shortly after watering. Before potting a plant, be sure it is dry and that the potting mix is also somewhat dry. Succulents are susceptible to rot from excessive moisture.

When you pot a succulent or cactus, set a large piece of broken pot over the drainage hole, then put a small mound of the prepared soil mixture in the container (to a depth of about 2 inches) and center the plant. If the plant is too high, take out some soil; if it is too low and the crown of the plant is below the rim of the pot, put in more soil. Fill in and around the roots with the prepared mix until the container is full. Settle this mixture by gently rapping the bottom of the pot on a hard surface, but do *not* pack the mix tightly in place. For species which are especially sensitive to excessive moisture (this includes most cactus), the top inch of soil may be replaced by an inch of gravel

HOW TO POT A CACTUS

Planting or replanting a cactus need not be the hazardous task that the spines suggest it might be. The drawing below illustrates the potting aid available to everyone: a folded newspaper. With this you can completely encircle the plant and lift it by holding the folded paper ends, or you may find it easier to grasp the plant with the folded paper between the plant and your hand. Heavy work gloves will allow you to handle most kinds gently without the spines penetrating to your hands. Kitchen tongs, too, can be especially helpful; those which hinge at the center and are oper-

ated like scissors are best.

A newspaper "chute" is the simplest convenience for filling soil in around the roots of a cactus you are repotting. This keeps hands far enough away from spines that the danger element is eliminated. Place a moderate amount of potting soil on a square of paper (at least 1 foot square), then grasp paper from the centers of opposite sides; the cross-section of the paper with soil will form a "U" or an inverted teardrop. From this paper chute, simply pour the soil into the pot around cactus roots.

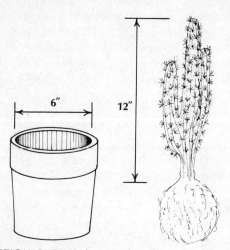

VERTICAL CACTUS plants are best planted in containers which have a diameter just half the height of the plant; pot should be deeper than wide.

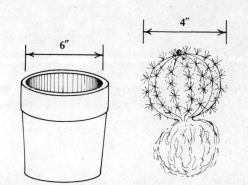

ROUNDED CACTUS plants require a container only 2 inches greater in diameter than that of the plant; smaller pots will be topheavy.

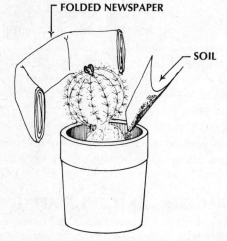

AVOID CACTUS SPINES by handling plants with folded newspaper. Potting soil can be safely poured around roots from a paper chute.

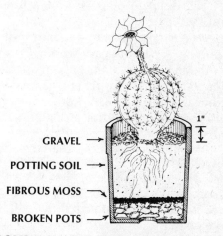
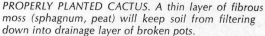

PROPERLY PLANTED CACTUS. A thin layer of fibrous moss (sphagnum, peat) will keep soil from filtering down into drainage layer of broken pots.

RECENTLY-ROOTED ECHEVERIA ready for repotting Soil in pot should just reach lowest leaves.

soil becomes caked and roots appear on the surface of the soil.

When you repot a plant, do not pull it from its container. Hold the pot upside down, rap the side sharply against a table edge and let the plant fall gently from the pot. The idea is to get the plant free with the root ball intact. Then gently crumble some of the old soil from the roots. The less shock a plant receives, the better it will adjust to transplanting.

It is sometimes difficult to remove plants from big tubs or boxes; it can be a tug of war with you the loser. You have two alternatives when plant and container refuse to separate. If the pot is somewhat soiled and unsightly—break it; it is better to lose a five dollar container than a ten year old plant. If a plant simply will not come out of a still-attractive container, dig out as much of the top soil as you can get—about 4 or 5 inches—and replace with fresh soil.

so that the base of the plant is not in contact with the potting soil.

Do not immediately water plants. Allow them to be dry for several days and then water sparingly for the first few weeks. This allows time for broken roots to heal which might otherwise rot with excessive moisture.

Cactus spines need not present a hazard in the process of potting. A pair of heavy work gloves is reasonable insurance against injury; even simpler is the use of a folded newspaper for handling a plant (see drawing on page 23); wood or metal tongs are also convenient aids for picking up and holding a cactus.

Repotting a succulent or cactus is best done in spring or fall. In spring, warm weather is on the way and plants have a chance to start growing. In fall, weather is still warm enough for them to adjust before colder weather arrives.

Generally, large plants in containers over 14 inches in diameter can grow satisfactorily for four or five years before they need repotting. Smaller plants need attention every second year, or when roots grow out the bottom of the pot, or when

WATERING

Many factors govern the watering schedule for succulents and cactus: the type of soil, the kind of pot, the plant itself. Succulents need more water than desert types. They can be watered all through spring and summer and about twice a month in fall and winter. Do not water plants (any kind) on cold days or on very gray days.

When you can see these plants growing, give them ample moisture, but when they are resting don't try to force them into growth. Use tepid water; cold water will shock plants. Specimens in large pots will not have to be watered as frequently as those in small containers. A large clay pot with soil holds moisture for several days; a small pot (5 inches or less) dries out in a day. Remember that clay pots dry out faster than plastic or glazed ones, and that plants in dry sunny locations or in areas constantly exposed to drying winds need more water than those in cool shady places. However, when in doubt, don't water.

FERTILIZERS AND THEIR APPLICATION

A regular fertilizer schedule is usually an important part of house plant care, but most succulents and cactus can grow satisfactorily without additional nutrients. A notable exception to this would be specimen plants in very large pots that are not repotted yearly or every second year; these will need nutrient applications at the proper times for continued vigor and good health.

Fertilize plants only when they are actively growing (usually in spring or summer) and not at all during the rest of the year. Many species must have a complete rest in winter, and any additional fertilizer at that time would harm them.

Bonemeal is a safe fertilizer for succulents and cactus and can be added at the rate of one teaspoon to each 6-inch pot. Or, if you wish, you can fertilize once a month during the growing season with a weak solution of a fertilizer having an approximate ratio of 10-5-5 (10 per cent nitrogen, 5 per cent phosphorus, and 5 per cent potassium).

YEARLY REST PERIOD

Plants, like people, require rest. At one time of the year (generally winter) many succulents and cactus must regain their strength for another period of growth. This lull in activity is essential to their health and a natural part of their life cycle.

During winter, water sparingly so that soil will definitely dry between application and move plants to a cool place, about 50°; some cactus require no more than a weekly light watering. Do not feed or disturb them during this period. If you do, there may be abnormal growth, susceptibility to rot, and a likelihood that the plants will not bloom the following spring or summer.

The rest period can last from a month to several months, and the plant itself gives you hints when regular watering and warmer temperatures are needed. You will see fresh growth starting, and the entire appearance of the plant perks up. Then it is time to resume watering and put plants in warmer places with more light.

Exceptions to the need for a winter rest period are the shade-loving and epiphytic cactus (like Christmas cactus species and hybrids, and epiphyllum) which have leaf-like stems, and most fleshy-leafed succulents which are not native to desert climates. These plants require regular watering throughout the year. Here, again, the plant's native habitat can be your guide to necessary seasonal fluctuations in moisture.

RESULT OF GOOD CARE are these handsome rosettes of Dudleya brittonii *and trailing* Graptopetalum paraguayense. *These require water throughout the year; sprinkling will wash off chalky powder on leaves.*

Indoors... a Variety of Uses

From window garden collections to specimens of living sculpture

SIMPLE DESIGN is outstanding feature of this dish garden; young jade plant (Crassula argentea) forms "tree".

Dish gardens, container plants, attractive landscapes, and terrarium curiosities are all part of the succulent and cactus world. In what other plant group can you find such an assortment of foliage shapes from green globes to finger-like forms to tree types? The patterns and colors of leaves or stems are amazingly varied, and the often-spectacular flowers—some like water lilies or daisies—appear in striking contrast to the fascinating plants. There is enough interest in these plants to make growing them a lifetime hobby. Whether you have a large plant room or a tiny spot at the window there are hundreds of succulents and cactus to fascinate you for years.

DISH GARDENS

If you are fond of desert scenes, it is easy to have one in your home. Succulents and cactus make ideal dish garden subjects: They are small and grow slowly, while other plants may soon become too big for a dish. These miniature landscapes offer great interest for little money and time. You can buy tiny gardens already planted from florists or make your own miniature landscapes. It takes only a few hours, and once the plants are established the dish garden grows almost untended.

Your first step in assembling a dish garden is to select a suitable dish. It can be any shape—round, square, rectangular—but it must have depth for at least 4 inches of soil. For desert gardens, a simple container is best; choose one that has color and texture that is complementary to the plants it will contain.

Many containers suitable for dish gardens do not have drainage holes, so there is always the danger of overwatering plants in them. In dishes without

FELTED, SCALLOPED LEAVES and knobby stems of Kalanchoe beharensis look best against plain background. Leaves may be 8 inches or more in length, half as wide.

CAREFULLY COMPOSED dish garden features cactus species grouped around large desert stone; soil is covered with gravel.

PLAIN WOODEN BOX with one or two carefully placed rocks can create display for succulents.

DAINTY DWARF sedum species are good companions for heavier plants; leaves are tiny, grayish to bronzy.

drainage holes put in a bed of small stones to provide a place for water to go, and then add some charcoal granules on top of the stones to keep the soil sweet. Over the stones place a thin layer of moss so soil will not sift down into the drainage bed.

Set the potted plants in the container and shift them around until you decide exactly where you want them. Your design work will be easier if you start with a dominating plant—an interestingly-formed cactus for example—and work around it with other plants. Use the textures, forms, and colors of plants to create a living picture. Put in soil to one-half inch of the rim of the dish and set plants in place. Do not water immediately; wait a few days and then give scanty moisture for a few weeks.

Watering—when and how much—is the secret to keeping the dish garden handsome. Soil that looks dry on the surface may be soggy underneath. Dig down with a spoon handle or your finger to be sure that water is really needed. Always apply moisture with great care; moisten the soil, never flood it.

A bright location where there is some daily sun will provide the best indoor environment for your dish garden. Plants will live for many months in a less-desirable place without much light, but of course they do not grow as well as you would like them to.

You can also grow desert plants in terrariums—glass bowls, brandy snifters, aquariums—partly filled with soil. These are often especially enjoyable to children who love having their own garden where they can watch plants grow every day. The glass garden is prepared in the same way as the dish garden but it will not need water as often.

Plants for Dish Gardens

Many of the succulents and cactus in this list are scale-model miniatures of some of the larger outdoor sorts.

Adromischus maculatus (calico hearts). Gray-green thick flat leaves, spotted brown; flowers tipped red-white.

Astrophytum myriostigma (bishop's cap). Gray-ribbed spineless oddity; yellow flowers.

Crassula schmidtii. Pointed gray-green leaves with dark spot; pink flowers.

SEVERAL KINDS OF CACTUS grow in dish at left; succulents at right (clockwise from top left) are: echeveria hybrid, Sempervivum arachnoideum, Sempervivum tectorum, and Echeveria elegans.

C. teres. Tightly packed column of pale green leaves.

Echeveria derenbergii (painted lady). Rosettes of pale green leaves with silver sheen; yellow and orange flowers.

E. elegans (Mexican snowball). Clustering rosette of light blue-green leaves frosted white.

Echinocereus melanocentrus. Small, spiny, dark green globe with large red flowers.

Echinopsis kermesiana. Round plant with ribs; lily-like red blooms.

Faucaria tigrina (tiger's jaws). Gray-green leaves with slender teeth, flecked with white; yellow flowers.

Gasteria liliputana. Mottled dark green and pale green leaves, spirally arranged.

Gymnocalycium mihanovichii (chin cactus). Gray-green globe with spines or "chins"; blooms at an early age.

Haworthia fasciata. Zebra-striped rosette of leaves.

Kalanchoe blossfeldiana. Fresh green leaves edged red; bright red blooms.

K. pumila. Sugar-frosted, notched leaves; red-violet flowers.

Kleinia pendula (inchworm plant). Gray-green jointed stems covered with tiny awl-shaped leaves.

K. repens. Cylindrical thick blue leaves.

Mammillaria bocasana (powder puff cactus). Globular, with snow white silky hairs and yellow flowers.

M. hahniana (old lady cactus). Globular, spiny, with long hairs; pink to red blooms.

Notocactus ottonis. Bristly red-brown spines, glossy green globe; bright yellow flowers.

Opuntia mammillata. Tree-like tiny cactus.

O. microdasys (bunny ears). Flat oval pads with tufts of hair.

Parodia aureispina (Tom Thumb cactus). Golden spines on a blue-green globe; orange flowers.

Rebutia kupperiana. Small gray globe; free blooming with red flowers.

R. miniscula. Bright green globe with red blooms.

Sedum dasyphyllum. Blue-gray leaves, hairy white flowers.

ANTIQUE PITCHER holds fleshy-leafed gasteria; for best drainage leave plant in clay pot inside pitcher.

SUNNY KITCHEN WINDOW usually provides enough light for dish gardens of cactus, succulents.

S. multiceps. Miniature "tree" with needle-like, dark green leaves; yellow flowers.

S. stahlii (coral beads). Reddish leaves closely-set together on branching stems.

Sempervivum arachnoideum (cobweb house-leek). Old standby: rosettes of gray-green hairy leaves laced together with silver webs.

S. montanum. Tightly-packed tiny leaf rosettes.

S. tectorum. Leafy rosettes; hairy stems.

WINDOW GARDENS

Generally, the small and medium-sized succulents and cactus are best suited for a window scene, while the larger types are better left for container accent or outdoor decoration. However, one or two large potted specimens can be set on the floor beside a window. Because succulent and cactus plants do not all bloom at the same time of the year, you can have flower color for several months if you use some care in selecting these plants.

Any exposure can be used—even a north window is fine for some crassulas and sedums—but east or south windows provide the best place to insure healthy plants. Most important, designate some out-of-sight place at home where there is some light and cooler temperatures for plants to rest. This is a vital part of successful succulent and cactus health. A pantry or an unheated but not freezing porch is a suitable place.

As winter approaches and plants begin to enter their rest period you should move them to a cooler location, ideally where the temperature remains around 50? The slowup or halt in plant growth will indicate to you just when this rest period begins. Many succulents will still need water but usually just enough to keep soil barely moist; some euphorbias and most cactus prefer occasional waterings with dry periods between applications. When growth resumes in spring, return plants to their spots at the window and begin watering regularly.

Succulents and cactus—unlike many other plants—are not fussy about the amount of moisture in the air. They perform well with about 10 to 20 per cent humidity, which is normal for most rooms. However, if humidity is *very* low in the growing area (less than 10 per cent), consider a

RELIABLE FAVORITE, jade plant (Crassula argentea) performs as well indoors as out. Companion plant is Aeonium canariense.

BASEMENT WINDOW GARDEN of cactus gives plants the conditions they require throughout the year: Light is plentiful and winter temperatures can lower just enough to provide the necessary rest period.

small space humidifier to furnish additional moisture.

Good air circulation is absolutely necessary for succulents and cactus; none of them thrive in a stuffy, hot atmosphere. Be sure the indoor garden is well ventilated, even in winter. Keep a window slightly open but not so open that there will be a direct draft on the plants.

A metal plant bin is another suitable place for succulents and cactus, or you can use a wooden box similar to an outdoor planter. While you can put plants directly into the box in a prepared soil mixture, it is usually better to fill the bin with an attractive, neutral material (peat moss, ground bark, or pebbles) and place the potted succulents and cactus into this material up to the container rims. This way you will not encounter the problem of waterlogged soil which is fatal to these plants.

Average home temperatures are fine for most species—about 75° during the day and ten degrees cooler at night. Most succulents and cactus will exist comfortably in areas that do not go below 45°. On severe nights, put some newspaper on the windows to protect plants from the cold.

Occasionally in summer, plants too close to the window glass may burn. A screen or a light curtain will provide adequate shading if you don't wish to move plants away from the window pane.

There is no great secret to watering indoor plants. Feel the soil: When it is dry to the touch, water it; then let the soil dry out between waterings. When you do water, soak plants thoroughly. Scanty waterings will form pockets of wet and dry soil.

Succulent Window Plants

A wide variety of growth forms and foliage colors is represented by the plants in this list.

Aeonium atropurpureum. Interesting form: dark maroon leaves in flattened rosette growth.

A. canariense. Large flattened rosettes of apple green leaves.

Agave filifera. Decorative narrow olive green leaves bear loose curled threads at the margins.

A. picta. Narrow pale green leaves with white margins; small black teeth.

A. victoriae-reginae. Striking plant with olive green leaves beautifully penciled with white edges.

Aloe nobilis. Pointed green leaves are edged with irregular white teeth; plant is a rosette on short stem.

A. striata. Stiff pointed leaves about 1/2 inch wide, gray-green with narrow pinkish edge; rosette growth on short trunk.

A. variegata. (partridge-breast aloe). Wavy bands of white markings on green leaves.

Cotyledon undulata (silver crown). Broad snowy leaves, beautifully fluted.

Crassula arborescens (silver dollar). Large silvery leaves with red margins and spots.

C. argentea (jade plant). Bright green rounded leaves suffused with red, shrubby growth.

C. cooperi. Low growing with narrow green leaves dotted red; dainty plants form mats of growth.

C. deltoidea (silver beads). Low growing with fleshy, white, triangular leaves.

Echeveria derenbergii (painted lady). Thick pale green rosette with red leaf margins.

E. elegans. Silver blue rosette, pink flowers.

E. haageana. Loose open rosette, leaves edged with pink.

E. pulvinata. Round hairy leaves, red flowers.

Epiphyllum (see pages 70-71).

Euphorbia lactea. Many-branched plant, the branches have 3-4 angles, spines, and whitish central stripe.

E. obesa (basketball plant). Multicolored globe.

E. milii (crown of thorns). Spiny stems with tiny dark green leaves and bright red flowers.

Gasteria verrucosa. Tapered pink and purple leaves with white warts.

Haworthia angustifolia. Light green rosettes of pointed leaves.

H. tessellata. Checkered lines on glossy green, pointed leaves; rosette growth.

Huernia pillansii (cockleburs). Thick green stems covered with green or purplish conical bristles; pale yellow, star-shaped flowers.

Kalanchoe fedtschenkoi. Blue-green leaves, clustered at top of stems; brownish-pink flowers.

K. tomentosa (panda plant). Tapered white felt leaves covered with brown dots.

Sedum adolphii. Short, fleshy, yellow-green leaves tinged red; sprawling plant.

S. multiceps. Miniature "tree" with needle-like, dark green leaves; yellow flowers.

WHITE FELTY HAIRS clothe fleshy, two-inch leaves of the panda plant (Kalanchoe tomentosa); marginal markings are dark brown..

ONLY A FOOT ACROSS, Agave victoriae-reginae *will maintain its compact, geometric form for many years before flowering, dying.*

Stapelia revoluta. Upright grower with ribbed stems; distinctive star-shaped flowers.

S. variegata. Finger-like stems with spotted, star-shaped flowers.

Cactus for Window Gardens

Most of these species have flowers quite large in proportion to the plants; often the spines are colorful as well. Most cactus flower in summer.

Astrophytum capricorne (goat's horn). Green globe with silver markings; 3-inch flowers are yellow with red throats.

A. ornatum (star cactus). Globular to columnar ribbed plants; both spines and blooms are yellow.

Cephalocereus palmeri (wooly torch). Hardy plant with short blue-green spines and tufts of white, wooly hair; columnar to branching.

C. polyanthus (Aztec column). Slow-growing, columnar with fluted ribs, yellow-brown spines.

C. senilis (old man cactus). Ribbed columnar growth, spines hidden in long white hairs.

Chamaecereus silvestrii (peanut cactus). Dense clusters of short green branches; red blooms.

C. Johnson hybrids (giant peanuts). Resemble a huge peanut; the large flowers range from orange to red.

Cleistocactus baumanii (scarlet bugler). Stiff stems topped with white spines; long blooming period of bright red, tubular flowers.

C. strausii (silver torch). Columnar clustering variety, silver-haired; dark red flowers.

Coryphantha poselgeriana. Blue-green, warty growth clusters, long stiff spines; large reddish-purple flowers.

Echinocactus grusonii (golden barrel). Straight, sharp yellow spines; with age develops a crown of yellow wool.

Echinocereus baileyi. Columnar growth, white spines; open faced flowers are generally yellow.

E. dasyacanthus (rainbow cactus). Small columnar plant covered with soft spines; large yellow blossoms.

E. ehrenbergii. Stem erect, free-branching from base with slender, glassy white spines; purple-red flowers.

E. reichenbachii (lace cactus). Small, heavily-spined plant with red and yellow flowers.

DWARF OPUNTIA species grow and flower well indoors; color range from yellow to red, the flowers appearing at the edges of rather flattened pads. Not all have spines; some have only tufts of bristles.

Mammillaria bocasana (powder puff cactus). Clustering growth, hooked central spine covered with white hair; small yellow flowers.

Notocactus haselbergii (scarlet ball). An early spring bloomer, globular growth covered with soft white spines; bright red blossoms.

N. mammulosus (lemon ball). Globular ribbed plant, gray to brown in color with short spines; yellow flowers.

N. ottonis (Indian head). Clustering globular plant with bristly red-brown spines; yellow flowers.

N. schumannianus (Paraguay ball). Globular growth, slanting at the top, with deep orange spines; yellow blooms.

N. scopa (silver ball). Globular, ribbed, covered with soft white spines; yellow flowers.

Opuntia basilaris (beaver tail). Upright blue-green growths from compact pads, withstands low temperatures; blooms range from pink to carmine.

O. microdasys (bunny ears). A favorite house plant, Mexican dwarf species with flat, oblong, spineless pads covered by tufts of golden bristles.

Parodia aureispina (Tom Thumb cactus). Small globular plant with golden spines; yellow flowers.

P. sanguiniflora. Small white-spined species, globular, with red flowers.

Rebutia miniscula (red crown). Clustering globular growth with green heads; large brick-red flowers.

R. senilis (fire crown). Dark green plant covered with a mass of snow white spines; blooms abundantly in brilliant red.

Rhipsalis paradoxa. Flat green leaves with saw-tooth edges; tiny white flowers.

Zygocactus (see page 77)

UNDER ARTIFICIAL LIGHT

Growing plants under artificial "sunshine" is a popular and inexpensive way to start seedlings. Where natural light is limited it is possible to have healthy, handsome indoor gardens by using artificial light over plants.

Fluorescent and incandescent lights are not by themselves miracle workers. Plants still require attention—perhaps more care under light than they do on window sills. Under lights they grow all year. Because a vital part of succulent and cactus growing involves resting plants at proper times, some

SIZE OF FLOWERS on young or naturally small cactus may approach the size of the plant.

YOUNG PLANTS of cephalocereus (background) and echinocactus species are small enough for indoors.

mature plants under light dislike the all-year growth period. Experienced hobbyists often can handle successfully mature specimens under artificial light, but the beginning succulent and cactus grower would be wise to experiment first with smaller plants before risking the investment in money and years of growth that many large specimens represent.

Many types of fluorescent lamps are manufactured: cool white, daylight, warm white, and tubes especially for growing plants. After years of research, most growers claim that a combination of fluorescent and incandescent light is needed for maximum plant growth. However, some hobbyists successfully grow plants only with fluorescent light; others use only incandescent .

One successful arrangement for succulents and cactus is two 40-watt cool white lamps, two 40-watt fluorescent lamps for plants, supplemented with incandescent light: 15 watts incandescent to 40 watts of fluorescent illumination. This combination is useful for starting seedlings and for handling mature plants that grow in winter when outdoor light is erratic.

With artificial lighting, it is important to distribute the light evenly. Reflectors or canopies painted white throw back light on the plants. You can use standard industrial fixtures (from electrical suppliers), or commercial plant stands with adjustable reflectors (available at plant suppliers). With these fixtures you slip the tubes in place and you are ready to grow plants.

There are a number of pre-fabricated light, reflector, and plant tray combinations that you can purchase; these range in size from two-lamp table models to floor carts with several shelves. With a little skill and imagination you can make your own lighting arrangements in the guise of bookcases or room dividers.

The duration of exposure to light determines the amount of food a plant produces and whether a plant will grow and bloom well. Generally, succulents and cactus need fourteen or more hours of light daily to prosper. Mature plants will need a considerable amount of light (intensity) and four or six lamps are recommended. Seedlings grow well under two lamps.

DECORATIVE CONTAINER PLANTS

Specimen succulents and cactus in decorative containers seldom fail to arouse interest where they can be viewed at close range. The sculptural growth patterns, the variety of leaf sizes, shapes, and arrangements are—in many kinds—combined with striking color patterns which contribute to the fascination of these plants.

The upright and tree types of succulents and cactus are especially effective in very large containers where their textures and colors can be enhanced by wood or tile floors. These same plants can be dramatically silhouetted against a light-colored wall. Groups of rosette-forming succulents (like echeverias) with their clusters of delicately scalloped leaves are particularly attractive in shallow containers on low tables where their patterns can be viewed from above.

Try to give these plants as much light as possible. If there is little natural light, put them near lamps or under overhead fixtures. Potted plants in shaded locations will have to be periodically returned to windows to keep them healthy.

SILVERY CROWN of Dudleya brittonii *with flower spikes tops this strawberry jar collection of succulents. Other plants are:* Sedum pachyphyllum, Crassula falcata, *and* Haworthia attenuata.

DURING WINTER AND SPRING, jade plant (Crassula argentea) will produce clusters of star-shaped pink flowers.

TWISTING STEMS and greenish flower structures of Euphorbia burmannii make striking contrast against dark backgrounds; stems die after flowering, new ones sprout from base.

LIGHTWEIGHT VOLCANIC ROCK forms naturalistic container for succulents. Plants grow in holes chiseled into rock, then filled with soil. Drainage is fast through pores in rock.

HOLIDAY PLANTER is shallow dish with Echeveria elegans arranged to form a tree shape. Plants will soon grow to fill the dish.

SHALLOW METAL DISH is piled high with a variety of succulents. Soil and decorative rocks are first formed into a mound in the dish, then succulents are planted.

SERIES OF METAL DISHES will give you terraces of plants in a flat area; echeverias, sedums, and sempervivums are low plants, Portulacaria afra provides height. Water carefully if there are no drainage holes.

Landscaping Ideas

Distinctive effects with little maintenance

DRAMATIC DESERT LANDSCAPE is brought into the garden by desert native, Agave americana.

The unusual shapes and varied forms of succulents and cactus make them outstanding candidates for achieving dramatic outdoor pictures—especially if you garden in California, Arizona, New Mexico, or Texas. Even where summers are short—in the Midwest, for example—potted plants sunk in the ground can add distinction to your garden during the warmer months. In severe climates these plants can be stored during the cold months in a greenhouse or on a protected porch.

The varied forms and shapes, textures, and leaf colors of succulents and cactus enable you to use large types as garden sculpture. A tall, columnar cereus silhouetted against a blue sky or a stucco wall can be a memorable sight. Palmlike yuccas and some of the sword-leafed agaves are bold and assertive. Echinocerei and the mounding mammillarias are effective where medium height and mass are needed, while the low-growing aeoniums and echeverias can create living carpets of never-ending handsome patterns on a hillside. In summer when the brilliant flowers of some ground-cover types appear, be ready for a spectacular display.

PLANTS FOR OUTDOORS

Cactus for outdoor growing can be separated into three types: the cereus type and its allies with thick branched and tree-like growth; globular or low-growing kinds including ball and melon shapes; and echinocactus—plants with a single, usually unbranched body in barrel or cylindrical shapes.

Succulents can be grouped into four basic growth types: the sword-shaped aloes and agaves, small shrub types (cotyledons and crassulas), those with rosette growth, and the ground cover plants.

EVENTUALLY A GIANT (to 18 feet), Aloe arborescens *displays flowers in yellow to red carried above gray-green, spiny leaves. Rosette ground cover at lower left is* Echeveria imbricata.

LUXURIANT PLANTING of succulents in variety is feature in this raised bed; low maintenance requirements are an outstanding advantage. Bold leaves of Agave attenuata stand out among others.

Planting the Permanent Landscape

If you wish to plan a garden of succulents and cactus exclusively, start with background plants and use large ones; they will be the frame for the picture. Torch cactus and yuccas are good candidates for this. For a desert appearance, the next step is to place groups of rocks, plant around them with medium-sized plants and in between them with small kinds. Feather-rock and lava rock are available at building material yards; while not really light weight they are easier to put in place than standard rock.

In the ground these plants (and especially cactus) need perfect drainage; therefore, a slope or raised bed is an ideal location for them. On level or nearly level ground where soil is any texture but light, dig a deep planting hole (at least 2 feet deep) and replace the excavated soil with a light, gritty soil mixture. After planting, cover the soil with a thin layer of crushed gravel or marble chips around the roots of the plants for frost protection. Be sure the location of this garden is in a sunny place.

Succulents and cactus grown outdoors take more water in summer than many gardeners realize. Where summers are rainless they may require water as often as every week. Because of cooler temperatures in spring and fall, plants do not require as much supplementary water then as they do in summer.

Outdoors it is important to harden and rest these plants by reducing moisture in fall and winter so they can withstand lower temperatures. It is not only cold that damages them: The combination of wet soil and soft growth is what makes the first freeze so hazardous.

It is difficult to determine the degrees of hardiness for each individual succulent or cactus because many factors are involved: age of plant, location in the garden, soil, and moisture. However, it is true that some species are inherently more susceptible to cold than are others. When it is possible, buy from local suppliers; you can be reasonably sure that their plants will survive in your area.

In climates with below-zero winter weather it is still possible to have succulent and cactus gardens outdoors if you grow the plants in pots. During the warmer months of the year you can sink the pots in the ground in your permanent landscape; when freezing temperatures threaten in fall, plants can be returned to cool indoor shelter for the winter.

The following list includes both succulents and

EPHEMERAL GARDEN DRAMA with 20-foot flower spike of mature agave; plant dies after blooming.

SHOWIEST OF SEDUMS is Sedum spectabile with flat clusters of pink flowers that bloom in September above blue-green stems and leaves. Shallow dish features sempervivum.

SPIKES OF RED flowers rise above narrow leaves of Aloe vera to punctuate planting of African daisies.

RETAINING WALL of concrete blocks on edge lets through soil to provide plant pockets for sempervivum.

GNARLED BRANCHES of an old Kalanchoe beharensis create distinctive patterns against light-colored wall.

LUMINOUS WHITE FLOWERS of Yucca recurvifolia are held in stiff candelabras above blue-gray leaves.

cactus around which you could build a landscape. These plants all feature bold or unusual forms.

Agave americana (Century plant). A 6-foot rosette packed with sword-shaped leaves having sharp teeth along the margins; indestructible.

A. attenuata. Big and bold, with soft gray-green, sword-shaped leaves in rosettes to 5 feet across; spineless.

A. filifera. Olive green leaves arranged in a circular rosette; curly threads at margins.

A. parryi huachucensis. Like granite sculpture, this rosette of tightly packed leaves has black spines at the edges.

Aloe africana. Tree-like aloe with long, narrow, pointed leaves; yellow to orange flowers.

A. plicatilis. Branching tree to 15 feet with rounded, tongue-shaped, closely-set leaves.

A. striata. Spineless gray-green leaves bordered red.

A. vera. Pointed gray-green leaves to 18 inches

long carried in rosettes on short stems; yellow flowers.

Carnegiea gigantea (saguaro). Tree-like with many ribs and stout branches curving upwards; slow, but eventually a giant.

Cereus hildmannianus. Tall and columnar, branching; large white flowers.

C. peruvianus (Peruvian torch). Treelike with blue-green branches and needle spines; white flowers, 6-7 inches long, at night.

Cleistocactus strausii (silver torch). Erect plant covered with white spines, branching at base with erect stems; dark red flowers.

Echinocactus grusonii (golden barrel). Big (to 4 feet high) and round, with golden yellow spines.

Echinocereus reichenbachii (lace cactus). Spines form a lacy covering over plant.

Euphorbia echinus. Branching upright growth, dark green with light gray spines.

E. grandicornis (cow horn). Angular contorted ribs with brown to gray spines.

DESERT LANDSCAPE is incorporated into home garden so that property lines are indistinct, house seems a part of the surrounding desert. Foreground planting features prickly pear and saguaro.

E. ingens. Tall growing, leafless and spiny; develops into inverted cone shape.

Ferocactus wislizenii (fishhook barrel cactus). Massive cylindrical plant with fierce spines; yellow flowers sometimes edged red.

Furcraea gigantea. Rosette of shiny green, narrow, spiny leaves to 7 feet long; similar to agave.

Kalanchoe beharensis (felt plant). Usually unbranched, a 4-10 foot plant with 8-inch triangular to lance-shaped leaves covered with white to tan hairs; leaf edges heavily waved and crimped.

Lemaireocereus marginatus. Spiny, tree-like growth with white-margined stems; to 20 feet at maturity.

L. thurberi (organpipe cactus). Ribbed, columnar cactus, sometimes branching from base, 15-20 feet tall, eventually; purplish flowers at night.

Opuntia basilaris (beavertail cactus). Low growing to 4 feet; leaves are flat oval pads, nearly spineless.

Pachycereus pringlei (elephant cactus) Columnar, with woody trunk and ribbed branches; to 25 feet.

Trichocereus spachianus. Strong, short, columnar growth; branches are parallel to main stem.

Yucca aloifolia (Spanish bayonet). Branching with stiff, dark green leaves that come to sharp points; single trunk or branched, to 10 feet.

Y. brevifolia (Joshua tree). Slow growth to 15-30 feet with heavy trunk, few branches; short, broad, sword-shaped leaves.

Y. elephantipes (Y. gigantea). For large gardens only: fast growing to 15-30 feet with several trunks; narrow, 4-foot leaves without spiny tip.

Y. glauca. Leaves $1\frac{1}{2}$-2 feet long, $\frac{1}{2}$ inch wide, margined with white on a nearly stemless plant; summer flowers are white.

Y. recurvifolia. Leaves are blue-gray-green, 2-3 feet long, 2 inches wide with harmless spine at tip; 6-10 feet, usually branchless with offsets at base to form a clump.

Y. whipplei (Our Lord's candle). Stemless, with dense cluster of gray-green, sharp-pointed leaves to 2 feet long; flowering stem 6-14 feet tall.

For Patio and Terrace

Tubbed succulents and cactus are easy to care for and make handsome accents in decorative pots in outdoor-living spaces. They can be used in pots on the patio or terrace; they can be in boxes located to relieve the monotony of a long house wall; or they can enliven entryways, driveways, or expanses of bare outdoor walls. The ball and melon shapes of many cactus make them highly desirable when something "different" is needed, and even one well-grown large agave or aloe in an ornamental tub can be a focal point of interest.

Patio plants are always on display; for this reason you should seek the unusual and most attractive plants for greatest interest and emphasis. A round cactus like *Notocactus leninghausii* or *Echinocactus grusonii* is especially suitable for a round tub. Aeoniums and bunny ears (*Opuntia microdasys*) are particularly suited to Spanish tapered pots. The organpipe cactus (*Lemaireocereus thurberi*) and various large agaves are other good prospects for distinctive containers.

Choice of a container is nearly limitless, but be sure the plant and its pot complement each other. Pay particular attention to scale: Neither plant nor container should overbalance the other.

Potted plants need a porous soil so that water can penetrate readily and drain away quickly. Sand is the basic element. Mix with equal parts of loam and topsoil and add some crushed brick to aid soil aeration. Feed outdoor plants monthly with a weak soluble fertilizer such as a 10-10-5 formula.

Plants in large pots can grow for many years without need for replanting, and in the meantime they require little attention. In summer, water them thoroughly about once a week, and in winter give them a suitable place indoors (where temperatures are around 50°) and keep the soil barely moist.

Planter boxes and border bins with succulents and cactus are often seen near house walls. This attractive arrangement is used frequently because plants need little maintenance. Generally, they are left in their pots and removed when cold weather starts. Aeoniums, aloes, and echeverias are favorite bin plants.

SEA OF AEONIUM DECORUM *edges this raised bed, contrasts sharply in texture with rosettes of* Agave attenuata *at base of tree.*

GRAY-GREEN ROSETTES of a young Agave americana are fine in containers; older plants in the garden will grow leaves to 6 feet long.

PLANTS GROW IN BARREL holes as they would from crevices in rocks in native locations; echeverias, sedums, and sempervivums are first choices for this treatment.

Ground Cover Plants

Many succulents are well-suited for low-maintenance, no-traffic ground covers. They spread rapidly, succeed in poor soil, and may provide brilliant summer color. In wall gardens, too, many kinds of succulents will find conditions to their liking and thrive for many years. In mild winter climates, ground cover succulents eliminate the expense of a lawn while decorating and holding a hill or slope.

The succulents popularly known as ice plants have a well-earned reputation as first-class ground covers. Many of these were formerly known as mesembryanthemums but have, in recent years, been separated into a number of different groups; these are listed, and their culture described, on page 74. Most of these plants will give you a showy flower display in spring or summer and attractive foliage all year. In addition to being decorative, both in and out of bloom, several species provide excellent erosion control on fairly steep slopes, and—because of their fleshy foliage—all are about as fire-resistant as plants can be.

Among the sedums there are also a number of fine ground-cover species. *Sedum acre* is a fast-spreading type with yellow flowers; *S. lydium* is a dwarf creeper with red-tipped leaves, white or pink blooms; and *S. sieboldii* is a popular pink-flowered trailer with 1-inch, round leaves. The Mexican sedum *(S. amecamecanum)* is a good yellow-flowered choice in cool-summer climates; for small areas, *S. rubrotinctum* will cover the ground with bronze-tinted leaves that resemble jelly beans.

Good candidates for ground covers are to be found in several species of kleinia; these have fleshy stems and thistle-like flowers. Perhaps the most popular is *Kleinia repens* with blue-green, cylindrical leaves. Similar but larger are *K. ficoides* and *K. mandraliscae*—from 12 to 18 inches tall.

THROUGHOUT THE YEAR, flowers decorate bank of ice plant Malephora luteola *which requires no maintenance other than watering, acts as erosion control. Red-flowered aloes grow at top of bank.*

YELLOW-FLOWERED Sedum rubrotinctum *with bronze-tinted leaves covers bare ground beneath planting of Agave attenuata.*

REPEATED PATTERN *of bronze-green rosettes of Sem-pervivum tectorum calcareum; covers small areas.*

MOUND *of Sedum amecamecanum grows equally well with little water at base of oak, much at lawn edge.*

SIMULATING A NATIVE CLIFFSIDE for sedums and sempervivums is a dry-set concrete retaining wall with soil between blocks.

SIMPLE BUT STATELY group of cereus cactus at left mark entrance to this desert home, will furnish large fragrant flowers in summer. Native desert yucca grows at right foreground.

CARPET OF AEONIUMS at left softens edge of stone steps in a garden devoted to succulents.

NEARLY SPINELESS beaver tail (Opuntia basilaris) makes rugged picture with desert boulder, gravel.

MASSIVE AND ASSERTIVE, two clumps of blue-green Agave americana grow in raised bed beside wide entry steps.

BOTANIC GARDENS can inspire landscape ideas. Here is group of southwest desert natives in natural setting with gravel and rock ground cover; rounded rosette is an agave.

CONTRAST IN COLOR and form is shown by three rosette-type succulents: chalky dudleya (top left) and two kinds of compact, green echeverias (right).

WEATHERED ROCK is congenial home for Sedum spathulifolium. Rosettes on short trailing stems are blue-green tinged reddish-purple.

CORAL PINK CANDELABRA of flowers (left) rises from broad gray-green leaves of Aloe striata to contrast with dark fence. Grayish Dudleya candida grows above grape stakes (right) which edge dry stream bed.

DRY STONE WALL is softened by plantings of succulents; soil in cracks between stones provides just enough foothold for roots. Two echeveria hybrids are large rosette clumps at left and right; small Sedum guatamalense with jelly-bean leaves is at lower right.

ROSETTES AND ROCKS go together naturally. The larger grayish-white plants are Echeveria elegans, (hen and chicks) to 4 inches across; smaller rosettes are Sempervivum tectorum (hen and chickens).

SUNNY PATIO GARDEN uses a variety of succulents for all-year interest and easy maintenance. Low plants in ground are mostly echeverias, aeoniums, and sedums; containers repeat their use.

BOLD SILHOUETTE against plain wall and open sky is created by a tree-like yucca growing among lava rocks. Leaf points are very sharp in some species.

Propagating Techniques

It's easy to multiply your favorite plants

NEWLY-ROOTED kalanchoe plants illustrate the range in size of cuttings which may be taken.

Succulents and cactus are often so prolific with offspring that in a short time you may find yourself with more plants than you can use. Even though you can buy nursery stock, there is something satisfying about propagating your own plants. Often rare or difficult species are nearly impossible to find, so multiplying your choice plants becomes the simplest—if not the only—means to obtain more of the same varieties.

There is little cost in propagating your own plants, and you do not need special equipment. You can grow succulents and cactus from seed, start them from cuttings, or graft them. Each method has different advantages. Sowing seed is inexpensive and you get many plants. The stock is generally clean and free of pests, and with certain varieties the only way to be sure of having the true form is to raise plants from seed. Taking cuttings for new plants is perhaps the easiest and most popular method of propagation. There is no waiting for months (or even years) for growth and bloom; some species from cuttings make blooming-size plants in a few months. Grafting plants is an exciting adventure in which you bring together two plants to grow as one.

NEW PLANTS FROM SEED

Start seeds in spring or very early summer so they will have a chance to grow before cold weather starts. If you will be growing many seedlings, sow them in wooden boxes or nursery flats; use shallow pots (azalea type) for small quantities of seed. A suitable growing mix is 2 parts soil, 1 part leaf

GASTERIA with fleshy basal leaves is one of many types which can be easily propagated from leaf cuttings. First, cut off outside leaf with shears or sharp knife.

CUT LEAF (from photograph above) into small pieces, mark which side is up, let dry for a week; insert (bottom edge down) in sandy rooting mix.

ROOT STEM CUTTINGS of succulents by taking 3-inch segments, let dry for a few days, plant in sandy mix.

DIVIDE sorts that form clumps of many crowns; each crown will root, be nucleus for new clump.

mold, and 2 parts clean, coarse sand. You can also use commercial packaged mixes like vermiculite to start seeds. Whatever you use, don't pack the potting mix tightly into the container—just gently firm it in place. Allow sufficient room at the top of the box or pot so there will be space for water.

A simple rule to follow when sowing seeds is to bury them twice the depth of their own diameter. Large seeds can be set in place by hand; smaller, dust-like seeds (like those of crassula or cotyledon) should be sprinkled on the surface of the soil. Put the seed pans in a warm (78°), bright place without sun and cover them with plastic or a sheet of glass. Whenever the covering sweats, allow some air into the container. During the germination period, keep the temperature constant and the pots or flats out of drafts.

The simplest, safest method to water seed pots is to set the pot in a pan of water and let water soak up into the potting soil. If you water from overhead be sure to use a very fine mist; otherwise, seeds will be disturbed and possibly washed from the container. The idea is to keep seeds evenly moist: Too much moisture and darkness brings on mildew; too little water and the plants will perish.

There is a considerable variation in the time it takes for seeds to germinate. Stapeliads appear in a few days, ice plant types take a few weeks, while a few cactus require almost a year. Germination depends on many factors—temperature, soil moisture, season, and climate.

Care After Germination

When seeds have germinated and leaves are apparent, give the new plants a little more light and remove the covering. Air and light are vital factors now. Too much air and light can cause them to burn, too little can cause fungus to grow on the soil surface—which will eventually rot the new plants. As the seedlings grow, give them more air and light. Keep soil evenly moist until leaves are up, then water somewhat less. Seedlings can be put into new containers of fresh soil mixture in about six months to a year from germination.

New seedlings are fragile, so when you take seedlings from their containers *handle with care.* Give them plenty of space in their new pots. Bottom watering is still recommended. When plants become crowded they can be lifted and put into larger containers.

OFFSETS form on old stem (left) of echeveria which was topped and the top re-rooted (see photo, page 24). When rosettes reach about 2 inches across, twist off, let callus for 4 days in shade, root in sandy mix.

If you would rather not use pots for sowing seeds, there are many other kinds of satisfactory containers. Plastic bread boxes are excellent, so are shallow casseroles with lids. Commercial small plastic greenhouses also make fine propagating boxes. Be sure that the container you use will allow water to drain through.

CUTTINGS

Take cuttings during the warm months just as plants start growth. Succulents and cactus may be increased easily by taking stem cuttings; these can be from the stem tip or from a section of stem that contains leaf nodes (this, for succulents only). Leaf cuttings can be used too—a whole leaf or sometimes only a part of a leaf; this is the easiest way to grow a new plant. For successful leaf cuttings, first dry the leaves for a few days and then place them in a light sandy soil for growth. Gasteria, kalanchoe, crassula, and haworthia are some examples of plants that can be easily propagated by leaf cuttings. If you have extra leaves and would like to experiment, put leaves in a jar of water containing a few charcoal chips; set this on a cool, shaded window sill. Many of these will root and may then be potted.

Cuttings also can be started in a shallow, well-drained pot or in a box that is at least 5 inches deep. Be sure the container you use has adequate drainage. Use a sandy rooting mix—3 parts sand to 1 part loam—and set the cuttings in place so they are in contact with the soil. Do not push them deeply into the soil. Keep containers slightly shaded and the soil just moist to the touch. When color and plumpness appear in the young plants—indicating that roots have formed—they can be potted individually.

Another way of getting more plants is by taking offsets; these are small plantlets that appear on flower stalks of aloes, agaves, haworthias, and crassulas. Many times offsets will appear at the base of a plant. Any offset can be put directly into a sandy soil where it will root.

Plants that form a dense mat usually consist of several crowns; these individual crowns can be severed with a knife or pulled off and each one planted by itself. Offsets and divisions both require the same basic treatment: warmth, shading from sun, a sandy mix, and even-but-moderate moisture.

FLOWERING STEM of rosette type succulents will provide material for starting many new plants. Cut flower stem into segments of 2 or 3 leaves each, let dry a few days, then place in sandy mix.

NEW PLANTS form at base of old leaves. When they get a little larger, twist them off, let them dry for a few days, then root in sandy mix.

TRIMMINGS from ice plant planting can be used to start new plants. Chop trimmings into small segments, scatter them on prepared soil like seed, and cover lightly with soil. Keep ground moist for rooting.

INCREASE KALANCHOE from leaves by making cut with knife one-third through leaf stalk; carefully tear rest of way, being sure to get bud at base of stalk. New plants (right) begin to develop in 10 weeks.

HOW TO GRAFT CACTUS

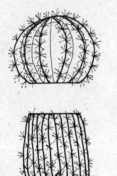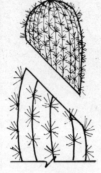

FLAT GRAFT   **CLEFT GRAFT**   **SIDE GRAFT**

THREE GRAFTING METHODS. Flat graft is easiest for rounded scions; flat scions (like epiphyllum) require the cleft graft; long, slender scions are best handled with a side graft.

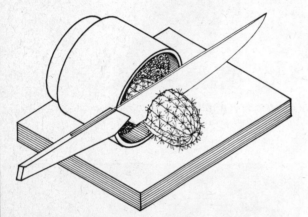

STEP 1. With a sharp knife, slice the top off the stock plant. A second, very thin slice may be made and left in place to keep cut surface moist.

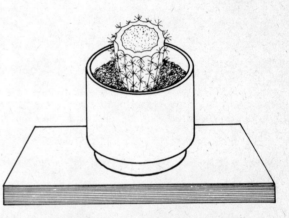

STEP 2. Trim down the shoulders of the stock. All exposed tissue of stock and scion must be perfectly clean to avoid rot.

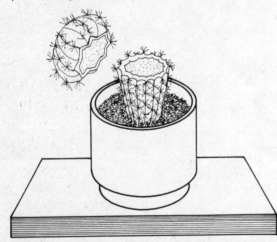

STEP 3. Inner growth rings of stock and scion must be the same diameter so they will successfully unite; if not matched, the graft will fail.

STEP 4. Remove thin slice (made in step 1) from stock and quickly apply scion, press them gently together. Secure scion in place with rubber bands.

GRAFTING TECHNIQUES

This is a somewhat more complicated way of producing more plants than is propagation from cuttings or seed. However, grafting offers the hobbyist several avenues of equally fascinating growing. The technique can be used to create or preserve plant oddities (crests and other unusual shapes), and it is also a way to get difficult plants to take root. In addition, grafted plants frequently grow more quickly and vigorously than if they were propagated from cuttings.

Not all succulents can be grafted; only members of the cactus, milkweed, and euphorbia families that have a definite cambium or growth layer will be successful. Grafting is best done during the growing season from May to October. It is then that plants are vigorous and with enough sap flowing to insure a perfect union of all parts.

There are three grafting methods: flat, cleft, and side. The flat graft is easiest—fitting a flat base to a flat top. After selecting the stock, make a transverse cut with a clean sharp knife on each plant, then press the two flat surfaces together. Use rubber bands, string, or toothpicks to hold the graft union in place. The cleft graft fits a wedge-shaped base into a "v" cut. Join the two pieces together with a spine or tie them with string. The third method is a side graft, in which both plants are cut on a slant and respective pieces joined with string until a union is formed.

Be sure the plant used as grafting stock is healthy and vigorous; it must support the scion until it is ready to be grown alone. Take plump, fresh scions from firm growing tips or new offshoots.

The success of grafting depends greatly upon fitting the cut surfaces evenly together so that the growth layers of both parts will be in contact with each other. Keep the cuts free of dirt and dust; if running sap becomes a problem, soak the parts in water for a few minutes to dissolve the sap.

Give grafted plants slight shade for a day or two. Thereafter, check occasionally to be sure the rubber bands or string are not too tight on the plant. Do not sprinkle newly grafted plants. Spines used to secure unions will dissolve within the plant without a trace; toothpicks will have to be removed later and will leave a slight scar.

GRAFTED CACTUS may exhibit combinations of forms not found in nature, depending upon the imagination of the propagator.

Troubleshooting Plant Problems

A well-cared-for plant will avoid most troubles

ROSETTE of Aeonium arboreum. *Contrast this healthy growth with that in the photo on next page.*

All plants at some time need attention for insect or disease attacks, but succulents and cactus are remarkably free from most plant ills. The very nature of their succulent stems and bodies make them tough and uninviting. Although insects *can* attack these plants it is a rare occurrence.

Good cultural practices are necessary for healthy plants, and a well-cared-for plant is seldom attacked by pests or disease. If a plant is not doing well, do not immediately think it is plagued with insects or the victim of a disease. Most likely, something is wrong with the plant's growing conditions. Check your culture first before you buy remedies.

Look for signs that indicate a plant is not getting the conditions it needs to prosper. Many times, these plants will perk up considerably simply by your moving them to another place; they may have been in a draft or in an area without enough light for a healthy existence. A gradual yellowing of the foliage, green stems that turn brown, abnormal elongated growth, or soft mushy growth—these are all physiological disturbances, the causes of which can be corrected easily.

The chart on the next page lists the most common problems that are associated with less-than-adequate care of succulents or cactus. Unless you can see insects on your plants that could be responsible for poor growth, you should first see if the signs of your plant's ill health are listed in the chart. The left-hand column presents a number of recognizable plant abnormalities; read across to the center column to find the cause, then across to the right-hand column for the remedy.

DAMAGE by aphids to rosette of Aeonium arboreum *shows most in new growth: leaves are small, twisted.*

PLANT PROBLEMS

SYMPTOM	PROBABLE CAUSE	REMEDY
Failure to make new growth	Too much water, or soil is compacted; roots may be decayed.	Repot in fresh soil mixture, adjust watering practices.
Stems or leaves are yellow	Plant is too dry and receives too much heat.	Provide better ventilation and more moisture in the air.
Stems or leaves *turn* yellow	Possible iron deficiency from soil being too alkaline.	Test pH of soil; add iron chelates if reaction is neutral to alkaline.
Pale color on new growth	Root injury.	Trim away dead or damaged roots, repot plant.
Elongated growth	Not enough light.	Move plant to location with more light.
Failure to bloom, or very few flowers produced	Plant has received too much nitrogen, or winter rest period has not been given, or both.	Use fertilizer low in nitrogen, higher in phosphorus; give plants winter rest (see page 25).
Flower buds drop	Temperature is too low or fluctuates too much; plant is in draft.	Move plant to warmer, draft-free location.
Soft or mushy growth	Too much moisture, temperature too low.	Reduce moisture, cut away soft parts and dust cuts with Captan.
Corky skin on stems	A natural development on some cactus as they age.	
Plant has glassy, translucent look beginning in fall or winter.	Frost damage.	No cure for damage done; keep plant dry; be sure it is not subjected to such low temperatures again.

DARK SPOTS on underside of these leaves are aphids. This is a light infestation and will not disfigure mature growth; if left unchecked, new leaves may be attacked and distorted (see photo on page 65).

IDENTIFYING PLANT PROBLEMS

Although the damage caused by common insect pests is easily recognizable, the insects are usually small and hard to see because they hide in leaf joints, flower buds, or in the soil. With many agaves and echeverias, for example, it is impossible to detect insects deep in the leaf axils of the rosettes. It is necessary to watch closely any plant that is not growing properly. Inspect plants at regular intervals; look for discolored leaves, deformed growth of new shoots—these signs indicate insects at work. If you do find insect pests, isolate the plant immediately so other members of your collection will not suffer.

It is important to determine just what kind of insect you are fighting before you can buy the appropriate remedy. There are some general insecticides that will take care of many kinds of insects but there are also preparations for specific insects. Know what you are fighting before you do battle. Many insects can be eradicated with soap and water. Nicotine sulfate is safe for indoor use and will eliminate mealy bugs and aphids.

Here is a list of some of the common insects that have been known to bother succulents and cactus.

Aphids. Probably the most common pest you will find on succulents, these small green-to-black, soft-bodied creatures dine on tender growing shoots and flower parts, distorting the young growth. Control: nicotine sulfate or malathion. Be sure plants are watered the day before applyiing the preparation and keep plants shaded for a few hours after you spray.

Mealy bugs. These insects cause extensive plant damage unless found early. Fuzzy white or gray and cottony, these insects are found on spines, stems, and roots of succulents. Control: Carefully spray with a solution of nicotine sulfate or malathion.

Scale. This is the most stubborn pest to eradicate. Scale appears as brown spots about the size of a pinhead; they have a hard-shell covering. Control: If the infestation is mild, scale can be picked off with a toothpick. For heavy attacks, use malathion as directed on the label of the container.

Root knot nematode. This microscopic round worm enters roots of plants and causes swellings that appear like beads on a string. They cause root

DEAD ROSETTES but healthy stems: plant may have been too shaded, attacked by mealy bugs.

CORK PATCHES on these kalanchoe leaves results from virus infection, weakens the plant. There is no cure.

systems to rot and, as a consequence, plants become stunted and pale in color. Control: Since these pests are introduced in soil, sometimes an infected plant can be saved by trimming the roots and repotting it.

Thrips and red spiders. Clues to their presence are small yellow or white spots on the leaves or stems of a plant. Control: spray with nicotine sulfate or malathion.

Snails and slugs. The work of these chewers is easily seen in holes and half-eaten leaves; fortunately, these pests are not difficult to destroy. Control: Use a metaldehyde bait; scatter it over the soil and then water.

Ants. Always try to keep ants under control, because they carry and help spread aphids from one plant to another. Control: malathion.

Fungus diseases. In plants, these usually result from poor growing conditions and plain carelessness. Overwatering, bruises, improperly healed cuts are a few ways decay can get started. Plants wilt, look wan, and refuse to grow. Open cuts and wounds on plants should be avoided, as these are invitations for disease to enter the plant and start

to work. Soft decayed areas and rot can also develop in the base of a plant from fungus infections. Control: Cut away the infected parts and destroy them, then dust the wounds with sulfur or a specific fungicide like captan.

To prevent disease and pests from getting into your collection, check all new plants carefully. If possible, isolate them for a few days to be sure they are clean. Set pots in a tub of water for a few hours to flush out soil-borne insects (see page 14).

Plants that receive good care are rarely attractive to insects; they are too healthy. It is the poorly-tended, weak plant that usually is the victim. Try to give all your plants a fighting chance by taking the best possible care of them. Do not, however, apply chemical insect controls unless you know that your plants do have an insect problem. Never follow the theory that if a little insecticide is good, a lot will be better; you may kill the plant. Always follow exactly all directions for chemicals.

Most important, guard children and pets against insecticides by putting cans or bottles on shelves where they cannot be reached. Never leave an open chemical container where a child can reach it.

Specialties

Some favorite plants of generations of collectors

RESEMBLING ORCHID CACTUS, this Hylocereus undatus *climbs with aerial roots, flowers at night.*

Even within so varied a group of plants as are found in succulents and cactus it is inevitable that certain groups of species and hybrids within these groups will emerge, in time, as favorite plants of collectors and home gardeners. Favorite plants with gardeners are often easily recognized by the number of named hybrids which are available. A particularly good example of this is the orchid cactus (epiphyllum) which numbers several thousand hybrids produced in over a hundred years of breeding with epiphyllum and related sorts.

Another means of designating a specialty is by noting the frequent *use* of a particular group of plants. The pages devoted to basket plants (pages 78-79) represent this sort of specialty; the plants listed and illustrated belong to many different genera, yet all are adaptable to a favorite garden situation. Ice plant species fall into this favorite-by-use category because of their extensive employment as ground covers, often as erosion control. Almost as a fringe benefit to their practical value is the wild display of color which many of them produce during the summer months.

A third specialty can be conveniently designated the "collector's item." Within this category are found plants which are treasured more for their distinct style rather than for the uninitiated's concept of beauty. Euphorbia species are a popular example of a collector's favorite. Most of the succulent plants in this genus are botanical oddities which have responded to difficult native environments in a number of highly specialized (often grotesque) ways.

REAL STONES are hard to distinguish from plants in this collection of living-rock succulents; daisy-like flowers in summer will break the disguise.

SYMMETRICAL FORM of Euphorbia meloformis is accentuated by reddish markings which run across the bright green plant surface. What look like spines are remains of stems.

EPIPHYLLUM (ORCHID CACTUS)

If you want something more than unusual foliage, try a few of the many eye-catching epiphyllum hybrids derived from rain-forest species of Central and South America. These spineless plants have flattened stems with scalloped edges and bear spectacular, large, saucer-like flowers in many colors. Nowhere else in the cactus group has such progress been made by hybridizers to achieve mammoth flowers in so many colors. There are over 3,000 named hybrids.

Epiphyllums are easy to grow and often look best when staked on a trellis or some support rather than left to their natural pendant growth. Give them filtered light and a well-drained sandy soil. They thrive in coolness at night (around 50°) and need about 60 per cent humidity. In winter, rest the plants and keep the soil just barely moist; they can be placed in an unheated (but not freezing) garage or porch. When they are in bloom in May and June, enjoy them indoors or outside where they can be viewed at close range.

While epiphyllums are easy to grow and bloom, there are a few tricks that will guarantee healthy plants. Pot them in small containers—they do better when the roots are crowded—and do not pamper them. Let them dry out thoroughly between waterings. If you want a good crop of flowers, make sure plants have plenty of light, but not direct sun. There will be scanty bloom, if any, in shade.

To some gardeners, the growth habit of epiphyllums is more a curiosity than a thing of beauty. However, their pendant stems contrast effectively with the growth of most other cacti, so that these plants may appear to advantage, when out of bloom, in a mixed collection.

EPIPHYLLUM HYBRID 'Mission Bell' has long pointed buds that open into brilliant orange-red flowers up to 6 inches wide. Throughout summer the flowers appear from sides of triangular or flattened stems.

WAXY WHITE, fragrant flowers up to 8 inches wide open from yellow buds on the epiphyllum hybrid 'Young Nun'.

DOZENS OF BLOOMS will decorate this well-grown epiphyllum hybrid during its flowering season from May through October. Hybrids with drooping stems lend themselves to hanging displays.

FLOWERING STONES

These plants are amazing replicas of tiny pebbles and stones—hardly like most familiar plants. Flowering stones inhabit the dry areas of South Africa where they have reduced themselves to two pairs of fleshy leaves that act as water reservoirs. They grow low on the ground and are somewhat rounded to conserve the greatest possible volume of moisture. Sunlight reaches the green cells through translucent window-like devices in the leaf tips. The form and coloring of these plants is a true miracle in mimicry. Without spines or teeth to keep them from being eaten by animals they simulate the rocks and stones where they grow so that it is difficult to see them on the ground. Only when they are in bloom are they easily recognized.

There are over 20 genera that have flowering stone plants. Perhaps the genus Pleiospilos is the most popular, in which the pairs of leaves are brownish gray or brownish green, angular in shape, and covered with dark raised spots. Plants are small—about 2 to 3 inches across—and grow in clusters. Some popular species are: *P. bolusi, P. nelii* and *P. magnipunctatas.*

Lithops is another genus of these remarkable plants, containing about seventy species. Small, conical, and only an inch or so high, they have a pair of fleshy, flat-topped leaves separated by a cleft. *Lithops dinteri, L. hallii,* and *L. karasmontana,* are some of the better-known species.

Plants in the genus Conophytum resemble the Lithops species but the leaves are joined with only a slight cleft at the top. There are rounded, cone shaped, and flat-sided plants ranging in size from 1/2-inch to 4 inches. Usually they are gray and have veins or marbling on the foliage. *C. minutum* and *C. giftbergensis* are attractive sorts worth trying.

Fenestraria species are desert dwellers where they are buried to their tops in sand. Because of less light and heat in cultivation, their leaves should not be buried or they may rot. During their summer growth period, water only moderately; hardly any water is required during winter.

Flowering stones grow best in a fine soil mixture of equal parts sand and soil. Be sure containers have ample drainage facilities because these plants will not tolerate stagnant soil. During cold or cloudy weather (and throughout winter), do not give them any water. Only when growth begins should water be applied and then only moderately, allowing the soil to dry out between waterings. Give flowering stones fresh air and some sun and keep where temperatures do not go below 50°.

EUPHORBIA

There are over 200 genera in the euphorbia family (sometimes called the spurge family), but the genus Euphorbia is best known with some 1,000 species. Some of them—especially the columnar and tree types—resemble cactus; many others are dwarf species, and there are also globe-shaped plants. Flowers are generally small and insignificant except in the popular crown of thorns *(Euphorbia milii)* and the Christmas poinsettia *(E. pulcherrima).*

Despite the variety and complexity of growth forms, euphorbias are amazingly easy to grow. They are fine decorative plants that will remain attractive for several years without special attention. While they may not be as gaudy as many other flowering plants nor as graceful in appearance, they offer beauty in their unique shapes.

Give euphorbias a bright place at the window and provide an open, well-drained soil kept moderately moist all year—except in winter when a dry rest of about six weeks is beneficial. The plants tolerate low humidity and a wide range of temperatures.

Because there are so many euphorbias, choose them carefully. Some are hardly worthwhile, others are first-class house or garden plants. Here are some attractive, popular kinds:

Euphorbia grandicornis. A decorative plant with whorling branches; stems are ribbed and the ribs are wavy with spines.

E. horrida. Looks like a barrel-shaped cactus with ribs and toothed crests; tough plant that takes neglect.

E. ingens. Candelabra type growth; stems have dark green wavy ribs.

E. mammillaris. A low plant with cylindrical ribbed stems; looks like a cactus.

E. milii (E. splendens). The popular crown of thorns with bright green leaves and vibrant red flowers; excellent house plant.

E. obesa (basketball plant). A perfectly-shaped round ball, gray-green with purple markings.

E. obovalifolia. A tall, branching plant with four-sided branches.

E. pulcherrima (poinsettia). The well-known Christmas plant; flowers (actually leafy bracts) are red, pink, or white.

E. submammillaris. A compact, branched plant with stems resembling corncobs.

THIS LIVING-ROCK PLANT, Conophytum placitum, *has individual segments which may be as much as 3 inches high and 2 inches wide. White flowers will emerge from cleft in each segment.*

TWISTED, SPINY BRANCHES *of* Euphorbia grandicornis *(left) suggest a cactus at first glance; another living-rock plant,* Fenestraria aurantiaca *(right), barely suggests a plant from a distance.*

ICE PLANTS

The ice plant succulents are mainly low-growing (to about 8 inches high) with bright, daisy-like flowers which come in many sizes and in all colors except blue. On overcast days the flowers close, but in sun they present a vivid carpet of color that can be seen for miles. In northern climates they are treated as annuals, but in mild-winter climates most are cared for as perennials.

The special values of ice plant succulents stem from their mass display of color in season and the ability of many species to control erosion. Their drawback is their general lack of winter hardiness, which limits outdoor usefulness to mild-winter climates. Most species, however, are attractive enough to be used as container plants wherever low temperatures would limit their use in the permanent landscape.

Although most kinds grow best within a mile or two of coastal waters, the majority will perform well in all but the hottest, frostiest inland regions. Carpobrotus species, *Cephalophyllum* 'Red Spike', and *Malephora crocea* will tolerate low desert climates. Unless heavy clay soil is your problem, no soil preparation is necessary for ice plants.

Shopping for ice plant can sometimes be a bewildering experience. Nurseries offer many kinds, and some are labeled only according to flower color. It is important to imagine how an ice plant will look out of bloom. Some of those that flower spectacularly have nondescript foliage during the rest of the year. Some of the most useful as ground covers have flowers that are hardly worth mentioning. The large-leafed types are generally too coarse to look at home in most gardens.

Consider also whether you're going to plant a slope or flat ground. Small-leafed or trailing types provide much better erosion control on hillsides than big-leafed or clump-forming types. If you plan only to grow and enjoy them in containers, then the amount and color of flowers will be your chief concern.

Ice plants have a deserved reputation for resisting drought, but they can not survive without any irrigation except near the ocean where fog provides moisture. Inland gardeners will need to water ice plant ground covers possibly as often as once a week during dry seasons.

Many of the plants once conveniently lumped together as mesembryanthemum are now classified under several different names. The following list will give you a brief summary of these groundcovers which are known as ice plants.

ROSEA ICE PLANT (drosanthemum) is lightweight, easy to root, will cling to steepest, rockiest slopes.

DESCRIPTIVE LIST OF ICE PLANTS

KIND OF ICE PLANT	IN BLOOM	OUT OF BLOOM	USES
SEA FIG *Carpobrotus chilensis* **HOTTENTOT FIG** *C. edulis*	Big but sparse flowers. Sea fig blooms purple; Hottentot fig, yellow to rose	Bulky, dark green mat of fat, fleshy, finger-length leaves. Coarse texture looks out of place in most gardens	Ubiquitous freeway ground cover. Great for binding loose sand at beach. Fine for large, flat expanses or gentle banks. But weight makes it a liability on slopes steeper than 1 to 4 (1 foot of drop in 4 horizontal feet); in rain it can slip, pull down topsoil with it
RED SPIKE ICE PLANT *Cephalophyllum* 'Red Spike' (often sold as *Cylindrophyllum speciosum*)	Brilliant early show of 2-inch cerise blooms, January to March	Pointed, gray-green leaves stick straight up. Plant forms clump 3 to 5 inches high	Use in small areas—along border, in parking strip, as pattern plant. Clumpy plants don't spread much, provide little erosion protection. Space 6 inches apart so plants fill in thickly
WHITE TRAILING ICE PLANT *Delosperma* 'Alba'	Scattering of small white flowers never amounts to much	Good dark green all year. Plants spread low, form sturdy 6 to 8-inch mat. Leaves are an inch long	First-rate for covering steep slopes or level ground. Runners spread rapidly, root, knit together to form strong, hill-holding network. Doesn't get woody or mound up. Foliage texture suits big or small areas
ROSEA ICE PLANT *Drosanthemum floribundum* and *D. hispidum*	Tiny but incredibly profuse flowers bloom in dazzling sheets, late spring and early summer. Pink to purple	Tiny, glistening, gray-green leaves. Long trailing stems root, form spongy, 6 to 8-inch mat	Lightweight, easy to root, can cling to steepest, rockiest slopes, can drape several feet over a wall. Also makes neat lawn substitute. One way to plant: just crumble or chop up stems, broadcast like seeds, cover with sand
BUSH-TYPE ICE PLANT *Lampranthus aurantiacus*	Brilliant flowers bloom early and heavily. Varieties are 'Glaucus' (yellow), 'Gold Nugget' (orange), 'Sunman' (gold)	Clumpy, erect plants look like foot-tall shrubs. Gray-green, 2-inch leaves	For low borders, gentle slopes, or where you'd use any dwarf flowering shrub. Clumpy growth makes it unsuitable for erosion control. Space 6 inches apart for quick, solid fill. Shearing in summer makes the planting neater
PURPLE ICE PLANT *Lampranthus productus*	Vivid purple flowers come in sheets early, last long. Can bloom before Christmas, last till May	Small, bronze-tipped leaves form solid 15-inch-high cover	Best on level areas, moderate slopes. Half-trailing, half-clumping plants don't provide dependable erosion control on steep banks
TRAILING ICE PLANT *Lampranthus spectabilis*	Spectacular flowers but season is short, dead flowers messy. Available in pink, rose pink, purple, red	Foliage never looks rich like some ice plants. Small gray-green leaves. Plants trail, grow foot tall. Pink variety has best foliage	Flowers alone justify planting, but it's also trustworthy ground cover on all but biggest, steepest slopes. Grow it where off-season untidiness won't be prominent
CROCEUM ICE PLANT *Malephora crocea* **YELLOW TRAILING ICE PLANT** *M. luteola* (both often sold as *Hymenocyclus*)	Sparse but long-blooming. *M. crocea* is reddish yellow; *M. c. purpureo-crocea*, salmon; *M. luteola*, yellow	Attractive year-round foliage. *M. luteola* has finer texture, best all-year foliage of ice plants	Popular freeway plants. Handsome ground covers for small or large flat areas, moderately steep slopes. *M. crocea* works on hillsides better than *M. luteola*, which doesn't send out long runners

GOLDEN 'SUNMAN' LAMPRANTHUS forms foot-tall clumps of gray-green foliage, is best in situations where you would want a low flowering shrub.

TRAILING ICE PLANT (Lampranthus spectabilis) covers itself with flowers each spring. Selected forms available with pink, red, or purple flowers.

CHRISTMAS CACTUS

These rewarding house plants have enjoyed generations of well-deserved popularity. They are difficult to forget, for in bloom they are a rainbow of color, the leaves barely discernible under a cloud of flowers. Zygocactus, Schlumbergera and their hybrids do not resemble cactus as we know them: They have no spines or hooks, and the dark green flattened stems are somewhat like orchid cactus—which are also from the same tropical rain forests where they share the trees with orchids and bromeliads.

At one time, the plants were included in the genus Epiphyllum, but unlike orchid cactus, flowers appear at the ends of the stems rather than from the sides and are smaller but more profuse. The blooms range from pea size to 1 inch across in white, cream, shades of orange, red, and fuchsia.

Give plants an equal mix of fir bark and soil in small containers. In fall and winter see that they have plenty of sun; bright light is enough during the rest of the year. Soil should be kept moderately moist except in fall when roots need dryness and plants require coolness (50°). Also in the fall, plants must have at least 12 hours of uninterrupted darkness daily for about six weeks to encourage budding. Any light which reaches the plant during a 12-hour dark period will interrupt or completely hinder bud formation. Once buds appear, regular watering may be resumed.

CHRISTMAS CACTUS flowers are about 2 inches long, appear in great numbers at ends of branches.

TWO-INCH FLOWERS of trailing ice plant (shown covering bank on preceding page) look like brilliant daisies, completely cover foliage during spring flowering.

MEXICAN GARDEN FAVORITE is the donkey tail (Sedum morganianum); *stems may eventually reach 6 feet.*

Basket Plants

Plants growing at eye level are often in a prime position to enjoy good light and admiration. Always a handsome display used indoors or out, there are many fine succulent plants for decorative baskets.

Plants in hanging containers need a moist soil, and outdoors during warm weather they may need water twice a day. Indoors, in less favorable conditions, water them about twice a week.

When you plant the basket, put several plants of the same kind into it for a lavish display. Baskets should be full, almost brimming over, to look their best.

Hylocereus and selenicereus species are, by nature, pendant growers. However, they are usually too large for basket growing under ordinary circumstances. Epiphyllums are also basket plants but do not always appear as attractive as other plants mentioned below. Zygocactus and Schlumbergera hybrids can be grown in baskets to make lovely colorful displays. Some other worthwhile basket plants are described in the following list.

Adromischus rotundifolius. Branching habit, oblong leaves covered with dots.

Aeonium caespitosum. Fresh green rosettes with reddish leaves; low growing.

A. decorum. Branching type with open rosettes of copper colored leaves.

A. haworthii. Bushy plant with trailing stems of gray-green rosettes.

Aporocactus flagelliformis (rat-tail cactus). Creeping pendant stems with reddish spines.

Ceropegia barkleyi. Oval green leaves with white veins.

C. woodii (rosary vine). Heart-shaped leaves marbled with silver.

Crassula deltoidea (silver beads). Tiny shrub with red stems and powdery gray leaves.

C. perforata (necklace vine). Pairs of bluish-gray leaves with red dots.

C. rupestris. Small, thick, gray-green leaves edged brown; trailing stems.

C. schmidtii. Gray-green needle-like leaves; brilliant rose-red flowers.

Echeveria glauca. Blue-green leaves tipped red; rosette plant with intense red flowers.

Hoya carnosa (wax plant). Elliptical fresh green leaves and whorls of waxy cream-white flowers.

Kalanchoe uniflora. Creeper, with bright green leaves.

Kleinia pendula. Gray-green, cylindrical, jointed stems with awl-shaped leaves.

K. rollianus. Masses of beadlike green strings.

Monanthes polyphylla. Light green plump leaves; small rosettes clustered together in cushions.

Rhipsalis paradoxa. Glossy green branches; zigzag pattern on leaves.

Sedum brevifolium. Tiny, waxy-white, round leaves.

S. dasyphyllum. Tiny blue-green flat leaves closely packed on stems.

S. morganianum (donkey tail). Popular basket plant with spindle-shaped yellow-green foliage on long, pendulous stems.

S. sieboldii. Creeper, with notched blue-gray leaves edged in red; pink flowers.

S. stahlii (coral beads). Spreading habit with dark green to brown foliage.

Senecio rowleyanus. (String of beads, string of pearls). Spherical leaves on long, trailing stems.

CRISP GRAYISH LEAVES and lavender flowers of Oscularia deltoides *completely hide hanging basket.*

FAVORITE BASKET PLANT *because of showy pink flower clusters and blue-gray leaves is* Sedum sieboldii.

INDEX
Boldface numbers refer to photographs